WHAT WORKS

William J. Bennett's Research About Teaching and Learning

⌇

Densia —
We thought this would be helpful
as we educate our daughter.
We love you and are so pleased
to have you in our neighborhood
Love,
John, Lois & Myra

edited, updated and with an introduction by

Dana B. Ciccone, Ph.D.
The Ohio State University

The Wooster Book Company
WOOSTER • OHIO

 The Wooster Book Company, Wooster Ohio 44691

Copyright © 1996 Dana B. Ciccone

Published in the United States of America

ISBN 1-888683-27-9

Library of Congress Cataloging-In-Publication Data

What works : William J. Bennett's research about teaching and learning. /
    edited, updated, and with an introduction by Dana B. Ciccone.
        p.   cm.
    Originally published: 2nd ed. Washington : U.S. Dept. of Education
    ISBN 1-888683-27-9 (pbk. : alk. paper)
    1. Public schools--United States.
    2. Education, Elementary--United States.
    3. Education, Secondary--United States.
    4. Education--Parent participation--United States.
    I. Bennett, William John, 1943–   . II. Ciccone, Dana B., 1948– .
    [LA217.2W52   1996]
    370' .973--dc20   96-41073
                                                      CIP

This book is printed on acid-free paper.

What Works:
William J. Bennett's Research About Teaching and Learning

Teaching and Learning Language Skills

Teaching and Learning Mathematics Skills

School

Introduction

Some years ago, then U.S. Secretary of Education, Dr. William J. Bennett, set out to make available to parents, educators and concerned citizens the useable conclusions from the latest and most comprehensive research in the field of education. This was his first charge in office and one that was successfully completed. The result of that effort, **What Works**, is unique in bringing to the general reader valuable ideas, insights, and information about the teaching and learning process. **What Works**, stands out as an immediately useable distillation of comprehensive scholarly research, field observation, and empirical study. The resultant information as presented in this very accessible format is the jumping off point for the kind of interactive involvement in the learning process that transcends both innate ability and socio-economic status. It is the kind of information that establishes the expectations and performance standards that are required of our school systems.

The subject of education and "what works" is a vast one. Key elements can be as straight forward as peer pressure or teacher enthusiasm. Often, however, the situation is complicated, convoluted and entrenched in bureaucracy. By involving the general reader—parent, teacher, and concerned citizen—in the process, and by sharing the key results of much scholarly study, **What Works** becomes a seminal reference work for the successful interaction between student and system, and between those outside the educational system and those within.

At the time of it's initial distribution, **What Works** was considered to be one of the crowning achievements of a national administration. President Ronald Reagan hailed it by saying that "**What Works** exemplifies the type of information the Federal government can and should provide." Putting this useable pamphlet in the hands of every citizen could further assure that the process of education – our most important and valuable investment in our own future – is also our highest priority and commitment.

WHAT WORKS undertakes to share the specific elements in the process that create valuable and viable educational environments. By involving all the concerned parties, the process of education becomes one of cultural leadership based on the mutual understanding that it is a combined commitment that will continually "improve the process" and continually improve the participants.

I would also like to extend my thanks to The Wooster Book Company for bringing this viable work forward and for their commitment in maintaining its availability. And to all the readers of **WHAT WORKS** for realizing that a commitment to education also requires homework for those outside the classroom. I can't think of a better place to begin.

Dana B. Ciccone, Ph.D.
former Director,
Office of Research & Senior Research Associate
College of Education
The Ohio State University
Columbus Ohio

Forward by William J. Bennett

UNLIKE MANY GOVERNMENT REPORTS, this report is addressed to the American people. It is intended to provide accurate and reliable information about *what works* in the education of our children, and it is meant to be useful to all of us – parents and taxpayers, teachers and legislators, newspaper reporters and newspaper readers, principals and school board members. But, first and foremost, this book is intended to be useful to the adult with a child – or grandchild, niece, stepchild, neighbor – in school or soon to enter school. It is designed to assist the adult who cares about the education of that child, both at home and in school.

The preparation of this report has been in my mind since the day, in 1985, when I was sworn in as Secretary of Education. In my first statement upon assuming this office, I said, "We must remember that education is not a dismal science. In education research, of course, there is much to find out, but education, despite efforts to make it so, is not essentially mysterious." In an interview shortly thereafter, I added that "I hope we can make sense about education and talk sense about education in terms that the American public can understand. I would like to demystify a lot of things that don't need to be mystifying. I would like specifically to have the best information available to the Department and therefore to the American people. ..."

The first and fundamental responsibility of the federal government in the field of education is to supply accurate and reliable information about education to the American people. The information in this volume is a distillation of a large body of scholarly research in the field of education. I trust it is a useful distillation. Of course, it is a selective one. It consists of discrete findings about teaching and learning that are applicable at home, in the classroom, and in the school. Many larger policy questions, many important education issues, are not addressed in this volume. And research on other important issues that could have been addressed was judged too preliminary or tentative to be included. But we now know certain things about teaching and learning as a result of the labors of the scholarly community. This book makes available to the American people a synthesis of some of that knowledge about education.

Primary responsibility for assembling the material in this report has been borne by Dr. Chester E. Finn, Jr., Assistant Secretary for Research and Improvement, and his staff. Immediately after Dr. Finn took his oath of office, I assigned him the preparation of this document as his first task. Many have contributed their ideas, knowledge, and energies, and I am grateful to them all. Beyond these individuals, though, we all have cause to be grateful to the scholarly community whose research is distilled here. We salute their accomplishments by paying them the highest possible compliment: taking their work seriously and trying to make it accessible to the American people. Many readers may find some of the research findings surprising. Most readers will, I think, judge that most of the evidence in this volume confirms common sense. So be it. Given the abuse common sense has taken in recent decades, particularly in the theory and practice of education, it is no small contribution if research can play a role in bringing more of it to American education. Indeed, the reinforcement these findings give to common sense should bolster our confidence that we, as a people, can act together to improve our schools.

I for one am confident that the American people are ready, willing, and able to improve their schools, and to assist their children to learn. The principal contribution that the federal government can make is to supply good information to the American people as they embark on this endeavor. Armed with good information, the American people can be trusted to fix their own schools. As this report makes clear, there is also much they can do at home.

This volume is not the only effort that the Department of Education is making to supply the American people with important, accurate, and useful information. We publish regular data compilations, such as the annual *Condition of Education*. We have produced pamphlets explaining to parents what parents can do to assist their children to acquire some of the basic academic skills. We have supported work by others that has yielded such exemplary reports as *Becoming a Nation of Readers* (the Report of the Commission on Reading, many of whose findings and conclusions are cited in this volume).

Nor do we intend to stop. I would, in fact, welcome suggestions for future efforts that would be helpful and informative, as well as comments and criticisms about this volume. For now, I am pleased to offer this volume to the American people. I believe that it represents an important step toward fulfilling the mandate of Congress, dating back to 1867, that the federal government should provide information to the people of the United States so as to "promote the cause of education throughout the country."

∾

Since we released *WHAT WORKS: RESEARCH ABOUT TEACHING AND LEARNING*, the Department of Education has been deluged with requests for the booklet. We have distributed more than half a million copies to parents and children, teachers and principals, scholars and policy-makers.

Editorials praising the book's clarity, good sense, and usefulness have appeared in newspapers from *The Christian Science Monitor* to the *New York Post*. Teachers have told us that it should be studied by every present and future member of their profession.

Unlike most education research – and many government reports – WHAT WORKS was addressed to the American people. It provides accurate and actionable information about what works in the education of our children, and it does so in a form that is accessible to all of us – parents and taxpayers, teachers and legislators, newspaper reporters and their readers, school principals and school board members. The information in WHAT WORKS is a distillation of a large body of scholarly research in the field of education.

The American people have responded favorably. An Ohio mother wrote: "My daughter is only 16 months old, but I feel your booklet has already given me ideas to help her learn more. I will be sure to read it again when she enters school."

The Chicago Board of Education, spurred by the WHAT WORKS finding documenting the benefit of homework has promulgated a policy requiring that all students be assigned homework every night.

Principals are using WHAT WORKS for staff development, professors for courses they teach. The booklet has been reprinted from Juneau, Alaska, to Albany, New York, by boards and departments of education, school districts and professional associations. The superintendent of schools in St. Paul, Minnesota, gave every one of his professional employees a complete copy of WHAT WORKS. The University of Texas used it to create a home learning guide for parents in both English and Spanish. The National Association of Secondary School Principals and the National School Boards Association also reproduced copies.

The Appalachia Educational Laboratory in Charleston, West Virginia, developed a workshop to train school personnel to use WHAT WORKS with administrators, teachers and parents. As a result, one elementary principal has begun sending home to parents written notices featuring a different finding from the booklet each week. Several teachers in the area have started inviting small groups of parents to the school for regular meetings to discuss some of the findings.

WHAT WORKS was even used as a Christmas stocking stuffer! A fifth grader from Kenmore, New York, wrote: "I would like a WHAT WORKS book. I would give it to my mom and dad for Christmas. Probably after they were through with it I would read it. I'm sure it would be a good book."

Clearly, the American people know a good thing when they see it, and we're heartened by that. But even though the response has been overwhelmingly positive, we have had our critics. They complain that WHAT WORKS tells only part of the story; that its real purpose is to divert attention from the Federal education budget; that it just rehashes old stuff that everybody already knows; and that it only helps white, middle class kids.

WHAT WORKS does leave some things out. It is not an encyclopedia; it was never meant to be. It simply tells a part of the story – maybe the most important part. (And this updated edition, with its additional findings, tells a larger part than the original volume did). As for the budget criticism, we will all differ on the appropriate level of Federal funding. But the fact remains, if we want to give our children a good education, we have to do the things described in WHAT WORKS. We can spend all the money in the world, yet if we do not do these kinds of things, we won't get the education results our youngsters need.

Some cavil that WHAT WORKS simply repeats things we've known for a long time. Common sense tells us that children improve their reading ability by reading a lot. True, but why are there so many students coming out of school who can barely read?

The fact that homework helps students learn is nothing new. Yet, why do one-third of our 9 year olds say they have no homework? Perhaps people need to be reminded of "what everyone knows"; common sense has to be reinforced and acted upon. Our purpose in WHAT WORKS is to make this happen so that our practices correspond to "what we do know."

Others mutter that this book leaves disadvantaged youngsters out in the cold. Quite the contrary. Many of the findings in WHAT WORKS come from "effective schools" research that was done primarily to determine what kinds of schools help poor, disadvantaged and minority children the most. We know these things can work for those children.

This is important because middle and upper class kids often manage to get by in life with a mediocre education. This is much less likely for disadvantaged youngsters; a good education is frequently their only ticket to a better life.

Many schools, located in desolate inner city neighborhoods, know and practice what works. Making sure that the lessons these schools can teach us become more widely known and followed is one of my top priorities.

In the meantime, I am confident the findings in this booklet can help all children learn more. I see evidence everyday that they really do work. For example, the Department of Education's recent study, *Japanese Education Today*, makes plain that many of the research findings in WHAT WORKS have been standard practice in Japan's education system for years. Parent involvement, clear school goals, high expectations – all discussed in WHAT WORKS – have contributed to the manifest success of Japanese schools.

When the first edition of WHAT WORKS was issued, I invited readers to send us comments and to suggest topics they would like to see in future books. This revised edition incorporates many of these suggestions, corrects a few errors, and updates some of the findings contained in the original publication.

We chose the new findings for this revised edition according to the same criteria by which the original findings were selected: they tell us things we can do at home, in classrooms and in schools to help our children learn more. And that, after all, is what education is all about.

Dr. Chester E. Finn, Jr., Assistant Secretary for Research and Improvement, and his staff prepared the original WHAT WORKS as well as this updated version. Many individuals inside and outside the Education Department have contributed their ideas, knowledge and energies. I am grateful to them all.

Education is not a dismal science, though many act as if it were. In education research, of course, there is still much to find out, but education is not essentially mysterious. One of my goals is to make sense of education and talk about it in terms that the American public can understand. We want to make the best information available to the American people.

This booklet is a significant part of that effort. It is, of course, entirely up to the reader to decide which parts of it, if any, to put into practice. All we can do is suggest that they do, in fact, work.

William J. Bennett
Co-Director Empower America
Distinguished Fellow, Heritage Foundation
former U.S. Secretary of Education &
Chairman of the National Endowment for the Humanities

WHAT WORKS

William J. Bennett's Research
About Teaching and Learning

Curriculum of the Home

Parents are their children's first and most influential teachers. What parents do to help their children learn is more important to academic success than how well-off the family is.

Parents can do many things at home to help their children succeed in school. Unfortunately, recent evidence indicates that many parents are doing much less than they might. For example, American mothers on average spend less than half an hour a day talking, explaining, or reading with their children. Fathers spend less than 15 minutes.

They can create a "curriculum of the home" that teaches their children what matters. They do this through their daily conversations, household routines, attention to school matters, and affectionate concern for their children's progress.

Conversation is important. Children learn to read, reason, and understand things better when their parents:
  • read, talk, and listen to them,
  • tell them stories, play games, share hobbies, and
  • discuss news, TV programs, and special events.
In order to enrich the "curriculum of the home," some parents:
  • provide books, supplies, and a special place for studying,
  • observe routine for meals, bedtime, and homework, and
  • monitor the amount of time spent watching TV and doing after-school jobs.
Parents stay aware of their children's lives at school when they:
  • discuss school events,
  • help children meet deadlines, and
  • talk with their children about school problems and successes.

Research on both gifted and disadvantaged children shows that home efforts can greatly improve student achievement. For example, when parents of disadvantaged children take the steps listed above, their children can do as well at school as the children of more affluent families.

READING TO CHILDREN

The best way for parents to help their children become better readers is to read to them even when they are very young. Children benefit most from reading aloud when they discuss stories, learn to identify letters and words, and talk about the meaning of words.

The specific skills required for reading come from direct experience with written language. At home, as in school, the more reading the better.

Parents can encourage their children's reading in many ways. Some tutor informally by pointing out letters and words on signs and containers. Others use more formal tools, such as workbooks. But children whose parents simply read to them perform as well as those whose parents use workbooks or have had training in teaching.

The conversation that goes with reading aloud to children is as important as the reading itself. When parents ask children only superficial questions about stories, or don't discuss the stories at all, their children do not achieve as well in reading as the children of parents who ask questions that require thinking and who relate the stories to everyday events. Kindergarten children who know a lot about written language usually have parents who believe that reading is important and who seize every opportunity to act on that conviction by reading to their children.

SPEAKING AND LISTENING

A good foundation in speaking and listening helps children become better readers.

When children learn to read, they are making a transition from spoken to written language. Reading instruction builds on conversational skills; the better children are at using spoken language, the more successfully they will learn to read written language. To succeed at reading, children need a basic vocabulary, some knowledge of the world around them, and the ability to talk about what they know. These skills enable children to understand written material more readily.

Research shows a strong connection between reading and listening. A child who is listening well shows it by being able to retell stories and repeat instructions. Children who are good listeners in kindergarten and first grade are likely to become successful readers by the third grade. Good fifth grade listeners are likely to do well on aptitude and achievement tests in high school.

Parents and teachers need to engage children in thoughtful discussions on all subjects – current events, nature, sports, hobbies, machines, family life, and emotions – in short, on anything that interests children. Such discussions should not be limited to reading selections that are part of classwork.

Conversing with children about the world around them will help them reflect on past experiences and on what they will see, do, and read about in the future.

Speaking English at school is especially important for children who have not grown up speaking English.

INDEPENDENT READING

Children improve their reading ability by reading a lot. Reading achievement is directly related to the amount of reading children do in school and outside.

Independent reading increases both vocabulary and reading fluency. Unlike using workbooks and performing computer drills, reading books gives children practice in the "whole act" of reading, that is, both in discovering the meanings of individual words and in grasping the meaning of an entire story. But American children do not spend much time reading independently at school or at home. In the average elementary school, for example, children spend just 7 to 8 minutes a day reading silently. At home, half of all fifth graders spend only 4 minutes a day reading. These same children spend an average of 130 minutes a day watching television.

Research shows that the amount of leisure time spent reading is directly related to children's reading comprehension, the size of their vocabularies, and the gains in their reading ability. Clearly, reading at home can be a powerful supplement to classwork. Parents can encourage leisure reading by making books an important part of the home, by giving books as presents, and by encouraging visits to the local library.

Another key to promoting independent reading is making books easily available to children through classroom libraries. Children in classrooms that have libraries read more, have better attitudes about reading, and make greater gains in reading comprehension than children in classrooms without libraries.

Early Writing

Children who are encouraged to draw and scribble "stories" at an early age will later learn to compose more easily, more effectively, and with greater confidence than children who do not have this encouragement.

Even toddlers, who can hardly hold a crayon or pencil, are eager to "write" long before they acquire the skills in kindergarten that formally prepare them to read and write.

Studies of very young children show that their carefully formed scrawls have meaning to them, and that this writing actually helps them develop language skills. Research suggests that the best way to help children at this stage of their development as writers is to respond to the ideas they are trying to express.

Very young children take the first steps toward writing by drawing and scribbling or, if they cannot use a pencil, they may use plastic or metal letters on a felt or magnetic board. Some pre-schoolers may write on toy typewriters; others may dictate stories into a tape recorder or to an adult, who writes them down and reads them back. For this reason, it is best to focus on the intended meaning of what very young children write, rather than on the appearance of the writing.

Children become more effective writers when parents and teachers encourage them to choose the topics they write about, then leave them alone to exercise their own creativity. The industriousness of such children has prompted one researcher to comment that they "violate the child labor laws."

COUNTING

A good way to teach children simple arithmetic is to build on their informal knowledge. This is why learning to count everyday objects is an effective basis for early arithmetic lessons.

Young children are comfortable with numbers; "math anxiety" comes in later years. Just watching the enjoyment children get from songs and nursery rhymes that involve counting is ample evidence of their natural ease. These early counting activities can set the stage for later, more formal exposure to arithmetic.

But counting is not limited to merely reciting strings of numbers. It also includes matching numbers to objects and reaching totals (for example, counting the number of apples sitting on the table). Children learn to do arithmetic by first mastering different counting strategies, beginning with rote counting (1, 2, 3, 4), and progressing to memorized computations (2 x 2 = 4). As children learn the facts of arithmetic, they also learn to combine those facts by using more sophisticated strategies. As their skills grow, they rely less and less on counting.

When teachers begin by using children's informal knowledge, then proceed to more complex operations, children learn more readily and enjoy it.

Television

Excessive television viewing is associated with low academic achievement. Moderate viewing, especially when supervised by parents, can help children learn.

Watching television more than 2 to 3 hours per day often hurts children's achievement in reading, writing, and mathematics, especially if it disrupts homework and leisure reading. More time spent viewing means less time for more intellectual activities. High achieving students, those with high educational and career aspirations, and those who are unlikely to participate in stimulating leisure activities such as sports and hobbies, are most likely to suffer.

Moderate TV viewing can, however, actually help students from backgrounds in which books, magazines, and other mind-enriching resources are in short supply. In such cases, television can expand children's horizons, introduce them to new concepts, give them information which would otherwise be inaccessible, stimulate their imaginations, and enlarge their vocabularies.

Parents and other adults influence how TV viewing affects children. Parents need to be aware of how much TV their children watch and how important it is to monitor their viewing time. When an adult selects and monitors a child's TV viewing – answering questions, explaining words, concepts, or twists and turns of the plot – the child's verbal, reading and writing skills often increase.

DEVELOPING TALENT

Many highly successful individuals have above-average but not extraordinary intelligence. Accomplishment in a particular activity is often more dependent upon hard work and self discipline than on innate ability.

High academic achievers are not necessarily born "smarter" than others, nor do people born with extraordinary abilities necessarily become highly accomplished individuals. Parents, teachers, coaches, and the individuals themselves can influence how much a mind or talent develops by fostering self-discipline and encouraging hard work. Most highly successful individuals have above-average but not exceptional intelligence. A high IQ seems less important than specializing in one area of endeavor, persevering, and developing the social skills required to lead and get along well with others.

Studies of accomplished musicians, athletes, and historical figures show that when they were children, they were competent, had good social and communication skills, and showed versatility as well as perseverance in practicing their skill over long periods. Most got along well with their peers and parents. They constantly nurtured their skills. And their efforts paid off.

Developing talent takes effort and concentration. These, as much as nature, are the foundation for success.

IDEALS

Belief in the value of hard work, the importance of personal responsibility, and the importance of education itself contributes to greater success in school.

The ideals that children hold have important implications for their school experiences. Children who believe in the value of hard work and responsibility and who attach importance to education are likely to have higher academic achievement and fewer disciplinary problems than those who do not have these ideals. They are also less likely to drop out of school. Such children are more likely to use their out-of-school time in ways that reinforce learning. For example, high school students who believe in hard work, responsibility, and the value of education spend about 3 more hours a week on homework than do other students. This is a significant difference since the average student spends only about 5 hours a week doing homework.

Parents can improve their children's chances for success by emphasizing the importance of education, hard work, and responsibility, and by encouraging their children's friendships with peers who have similar values. The ideals that students, their parents, and their peers hold are more important than a student's socio-economic and ethnic background in predicting academic success.

GETTING PARENTS INVOLVED

Parental involvement helps children learn more effectively. Teachers who are successful at involving parents in their children's schoolwork are successful because they work at it.

Most parents want to be involved with their children's schoolwork but are unsure of what to do or how to do it. Many say they would welcome more guidance and ideas from teachers. But it takes more than occasional parent-teacher conferences and school open houses to involve parents. Teachers who are successful at promoting parent participation in the early grades use strategies like these:

- Some teachers ask parents to read aloud to the child, to listen to the child read, and to sign homework papers.
- Others encourage parents to drill students on math and spelling and to help with homework lessons.
- Teachers also encourage parents to discuss school activities with their children and suggest ways parents can help teach their children at home. For example, a simple home activity might be alphabetizing books; a more complex one would be using kitchen supplies in an elementary science experiment.
- Teachers also send home suggestions for games or group activities related to the child's schoolwork that parent and child can play together.

Teachers meet parents' wishes for face-to-face contact by inviting them to the classroom to see how their children are being taught. This first-hand observation shows parents how the teacher teaches and gives parents ideas on what they can do at home.

Cooperative Learning

Students in cooperative learning teams learn to work toward a common goal, help one another learn, gain self-esteem, take more responsibility for their own learning, and come to respect and like their classmates.

Cooperative learning refers to assigning students to small teams – usually with four or five members. Each team approximates the overall composition of the class by mixing high and low achievers, male and female students, etc.

Several cooperative learning methods increase student achievement. For example, the teacher may present a lesson and then have students work in teams to master the material. Students are then quizzed individually and teams earn certificates or other recognition based on their team averages. Another effective method uses a group project approach, primarily in social studies. Groups plan learning activities together, divide tasks among themselves, and carry out their study plans, finally presenting a display or report to the class.

Although cooperative learning methods differ, those that consistently increase student achievement share two features. First, a group goal or reward is provided so that students must work together to succeed as a group. Second, group success depends on the individual learning of each group member, not on a single group product.

In cooperative learning, students encourage one another to do their best and help one another learn. High, average, and low achievers gain equally from cooperative learning. Low achievers contribute and experience success in academic work. Bright students deepen their understanding of concepts by explaining them to others. Discussions take place that promote critical thinking. And students learn the valuable skill of cooperating with others to achieve a common goal.

ILLUSTRATIONS

Well chosen diagrams, graphs, photos and illustrations can enhance students' learning.

Illustrations that accompany text help students understand written information and remember it later. Specific kinds of pictures help students of all ages and levels of ability, especially those with learning difficulties.

Different types of illustrations serve different purposes. Some enhance students' initial understanding of written information. Others clarify the meaning of complex concepts, while still others provide images that fix designated content firmly in students' memory. For example, an illustration of an octagon clarifies the definition of the figure as a polygon with eight equal angles and eight uniform sides; a photo of a town severely damaged by an earthquake depicts the devastation far better than words alone; an illustration can help students' understand the concept that fractions are part of a whole:

> George and his twin sisters cut a pizza in 12 equal pieces and each of them then ate one-fourth of the pizza. How many pieces were left?

On the other hand, mere inclusion in the text of a portrait of an historical figure is just window dressing It may even be distracting, especially for students who lack basic reading skills. For these students, pictures with little textual value may inhibit the development of independent reading and comprehension skills.

It is important to distinguish among illustrations and their relationships to lessons being taught. Those that enhance the text or create supplementary images aid learning, while those not related to the text impede learning.

TEACHER EXPECTATIONS

Teachers who set and communicate high expectations to all their students obtain greater academic performance from those students than teachers who set low expectations.

The expectations teachers have about what students can and cannot learn may become self-fulfilling prophecies. Students tend to learn as little – or as much – as their teachers expect.

Students from whom teachers expect less are treated differently. Such students typically:
• are seated farther away from the teacher,
• receive less direct instruction,
• have fewer opportunities to learn new material, and
• are asked to do less work.

Teachers also call on these students less often and the questions they ask are more likely to be simple and basic than thought provoking. Typically, such students are given less time to respond and less help when their answers are wrong. But when teachers give these same students the chance to answer more challenging questions, the students contribute more ideas and opinions to class discussions.

STUDENT ABILITY AND EFFORT

Children's understanding of the relationship between being smart and hard work changes as they grow.

When children start school, they think that ability and effort are the same thing; in other words, they believe that if they work hard they will become smart. Thus, younger children who fail believe this is because they didn't try hard enough, not because they have less ability.

Because teachers tend to reward effort in earlier grades, children frequently concentrate on working hard rather than on the quality of their work. As a result, they may not learn how to judge how well they are performing.

In later elementary grades, students slowly learn that ability and effort are not the same. They come to believe that lower ability requires harder work to keep up and that students with higher ability need not work so hard. At this stage, speed at completing tasks replaces effort as the sign of ability; high levels of effort may even carry the stigma of low ability.

Consequently, many secondary school students, despite their ability, will not expend the effort needed to achieve their potential. Under achievement can become a way of life.

Once students begin believing they have failed because they lack ability, they tend to lose hope for future success. They develop a pattern of academic hopelessness and stop trying. They see academic obstacles as insurmountable and devote less effort to learning.

Teachers who are alert to these beliefs in youngsters will keep their students motivated and on task. They will also slowly nudge their students toward the realism of judging themselves by performance. For example, teachers will set high expectations and insist that students put forth the effort required to meet the school's academic standards. They will make sure slower learners are rewarded for their progress and abler students are challenged according to their abilities.

ATTAINING COMPETENCE

As students acquire knowledge and skill, their thinking and reasoning take on distinct characteristics. Teachers who are alert to these changes can determine how well their students are progressing toward becoming competent thinkers and problem solvers.

- The isolated ideas and initial explanations with which students begin to learn a new topic become integrated and more widely applicable. For example, children just beginning to learn about dinosaurs tend to classify them in terms of visible characteristics, such as size and skin texture. Children who are more familiar with dinosaurs make more elaborate classifications in which sensory features become less important than more abstract features such as dietary habits.
- When confronting problems, competent learners identify fundamental principles that allow them to reach solutions smoothly, instead of wrestling with details. Where beginning physics students tend to classify problems in terms of surface features, more accomplished learners classify the same problems in terms of underlying physical principles. For example, beginning students view problems in mechanics as involving inclined planes and pulleys; more competent learners see the same problems as involving mechanical principles such as conservation of energy.
- Besides grasping rules and principles, competent learners are aware of the range of conditions under which these principles apply. In the example mentioned above, accomplished learners not only understand the principle of conservation of energy, but are also aware of problems that can be solved using such principles.
- Tasks that beginning students carry out with concentration are performed automatically by students with more expertise. This frees them to direct their attention to analysis, critical thinking, and other demanding aspects of performance. For example, when children first learn to read, they must devote much attention to the

process of translating printed letters into pronounceable words. As their expertise increases, children more quickly and accurately recognize printed words. This frees them to devote more attention to grasping the meanings conveyed by the text.

- By monitoring these changes, students and teachers can assess progress toward competence.

MANAGING CLASSROOM TIME

How much time students are actively engaged in learning contributes strongly to their achievement. The amount of time available for learning is determined by the instructional and management skills of the teacher and the priorities set by the school administration.

Teachers must not only know the subjects they teach, they must also be effective classroom managers. Studies of elementary school teachers have found that the amount of time the teachers actually used for instruction varied between 50 and 90 percent of the total school time available to them.

Effective time managers in the classroom do not waste valuable minutes on unimportant activities; they keep their students continuously and actively engaged. Good managers perform the following time conserving functions:

• *Planning Class Work*: choosing the content to be studied, scheduling time for presentation and study, and choosing those instructional activities (such as grouping, seatwork, or recitation) best suited to learning the material at hand;

• *Communicating Goals*: setting and conveying expectations so students know what they are to do, what it will take to get a passing grade, and what the consequences of failure will be;

• *Regulating Learning Activities*: sequencing course content so knowledge builds on itself, pacing instruction so students are prepared for the next step, monitoring success rates so all students stay productively engaged regardless of how quickly they learn, and running an orderly, academically focused classroom that keeps wasted time and misbehavior to a minimum.

When teachers carry out these functions successfully and supplement them with a well-designed and well-managed program of homework, they can achieve three important goals:

• They capture students' attention.

• They make the best use of available learning time.

• They encourage academic achievement.

BEHAVIOR PROBLEMS

Good classroom management is essential for teachers to deal with students who chronically misbehave, but such students also benefit from specific suggestions from teachers on how to cope with their conflicts and frustrations. This also helps them gain insights about their behavior.

Problem students are those who consistently underachieve, are hostile, aggressive, defiant, hyperactive, easily distracted, socially withdrawn or rejected by other students. Many of these students don't know how to socialize with others in acceptable ways.

Teachers who successfully help problem students use several strategies. Along with enforcing simple discipline and providing alternative services when necessary, these teachers set and enforce limits in order to gain control over the problem student's behavior. Such limits are set to help these students learn to control themselves and to create an orderly atmosphere for other students, not to exact retribution.

Teachers also suggest ways the students can cope with problem situations, communicate positive expectations for improvement, and reinforce good behavior. They seek friendly personal relationships with the students, help them develop a sense of right and wrong, and encourage them to empathize with others. They also use counseling techniques to help the students understand why their behavior is troublesome.

These teachers are confident they can significantly improve the student's behavior if they invest the necessary time and effort. They make it their business to work personally with the students. They ask the parents, principal, or the school's mental health specialist (counselor, psychologist or social worker) to supplement their efforts, but not to assume total responsibility. The teacher remains engaged, too.

Direct Instruction

When teachers explain exactly what students are expected to learn, and demonstrate the steps needed to accomplish a particular academic task, students learn more.

The procedure stated above is called "direct instruction." It is based on the assumption that knowing how to learn may not come naturally to all students, especially to beginning and low ability learners. Direct instruction takes children through learning steps systematically, helping them see both the purpose and the result of each step. In this way, children learn not only a lesson's content but also a method for learning that content.

The basic components of direct instruction are:

• setting clear goals for students and making sure they understand those goals,
• presenting a sequence of well-organized assignments,
• giving students clear, concise explanations and illustrations of the subject matter,
• asking frequent questions to see if children understand the work, and
• giving students frequent opportunities to practice what they have learned.

Direct instruction does not mean repetition. It does mean leading students through a process and teaching them to use that process as a skill to master other academic tasks. Direct instruction has been particularly effective in teaching basic skills to young and disadvantaged children, as well as in helping older and higher ability students to master more complex materials and to develop independent study skills.

TEACHER FEEDBACK

Constructive feedback from teachers, including deserved praise and specific suggestions, helps students learn, as well as develop positive self-esteem.

Teachers should not underestimate the impact of constructive feedback on their students. Providing positive and timely comments is a practice that teachers at all levels can use. These comments help students correct errors and give them recognition when deserved. Helpful feedback praises successful aspects of a student's work and points out those areas that need improvement.

Useful feedback, whether positive or negative, is prompt, germane, and includes specific observations and recommendations. It tells students what they are doing, how they are doing it, and how they can improve. Whether written or spoken, effective feedback is initiated by the teacher and is given privately rather than in front of the class. An example of effective feedback is: "Your book report is well written, Paul. The content is clear because the ideas are presented in a logical order and the details support your main idea. Your use of some clever examples makes your book report enjoyable to read. Next time, let's work harder to organize your time so that you will meet the assigned deadline." An example of ineffective feedback is: "Your book report is well written, Paul. But it is late and I'm upset about that."

Students who are accustomed to failure and who have difficulty mastering skills react more positively to encouragement and praise from teachers than to criticism. Effective teachers successfully use praise to motivate their low-achieving students. On the other hand, higher achieving students respond more to specific comments and suggestions about their work.

Through constructive, timely feedback, teachers can reinforce and help develop positive self-esteem in their students. Students who believe they can succeed are usually more successful than those with low self-esteem when it comes to participating in activities, working independently, getting along with others, and achieving academically.

Tutoring

Students tutoring other students can lead to improved academic achievement for both student and tutor, and to positive attitudes toward course work.

Tutoring programs consistently raise the achievement of both the students receiving instruction and those providing it. Peer tutoring, when used as a supplement to regular classroom teaching, helps slow and underachieving students master their lessons and succeed in school. Preparing and giving the lessons also benefits the tutors themselves because they learn more about the material they are teaching.

Of the tutoring programs that have been studied, the most effective include the following elements:
• highly structured and well-planned curricula and instructional methods,
• instruction in basic content and skills (first grade through third grade), especially in arithmetic, and
• a relatively short duration of instruction (a few weeks or months).

When these features were combined in the same program, the students being tutored not only learned more than they did without tutoring, they also developed a more positive attitude about what they were studying. Their tutors also learned more than students who did not tutor.

MEMORIZATION

Memorizing can help students absorb and retain the factual information on which understanding and critical thought are based.

Most children at some time memorize multiplication tables, the correct spelling of words, historical dates, and passages of literature such as the poetry of Robert Frost or the sonnets of Shakespeare. Memorizing simplifies the process of recalling information and allows its use to become automatic. Understanding and critical thought can then build on this base of knowledge and fact. Indeed, the more sophisticated mental operations of analysis, synthesis, and evaluation are impossible without rapid and accurate recall of bodies of specific knowledge.

Teachers can encourage students to develop memory skills by teaching highly structured and carefully sequenced lessons, with frequent reinforcement for correct answers. Young students, slow students, and students who lack background knowledge can benefit from such instruction.

In addition, teachers can teach *mnemonics*, that is, devices and techniques for improving memory. For example, the mnemonic "Every Good Boy Does Fine" has reminded generations of music students that E, G, B, D, and F are the notes to which the lines on a treble staff correspond. Mnemonics helps students remember more information faster and retain it longer. Comprehension and retention are even greater when teachers and students connect the new information being memorized with previous knowledge.

QUESTIONING

Student achievement rises when teachers ask questions that require students to apply, analyze, synthesize, and evaluate information in addition to simply recalling facts.

Even before Socrates, questioning was one of teaching's most common and most effective techniques. Some teachers ask hundreds of questions, especially when teaching science, geography, history, or literature.

But questions take different forms and place different demands on students. Some questions require only factual recall and do not provoke analysis. For example, of more than 61,000 questions found in the teacher guides, student workbooks, and tests for nine history textbooks, more than ninety-five percent were devoted to factual recall. This is not to say that questions meant to elicit facts are unimportant. Students need basic information to engage in higher level thinking processes and discussions. Such questions also promote class participation and provide a high success rate in answering questions correctly.

The difference between factual and thought-provoking questions is the difference between asking: "When did Lincoln deliver the Gettysburg Address?" and asking: "Why was Lincoln's Gettysburg Address an important speech?" Each kind of question has its place, but the second one intends that the student analyze the speech in terms of the issues of the Civil War.

Although both kinds of questions are important, students achieve more when teachers ask thought-provoking questions and insist on thoughtful answers. Students' answers may also improve if teachers wait longer for a response, giving students more time to think.

STUDY SKILLS

The ways in which children study, influence strongly how much they learn. Teachers can often help children develop better study skills.

Research has identified several study skills used by good students that can be taught to other students. Average students can learn how to use these skills. Low ability students may need to be taught when, as well as how, to use them.

Here are some examples of sound study practices:

- Good students adjust the way they study according to several factors:
  - the demand of the material,
  - the time available for studying,
  - what they already know about the topic,
  - the purpose and importance of the assignment, and
  - the standards they must meet.
- Good students space learning sessions on a topic over time and do not cram or study the same topic continuously.
- Good students identify the main idea in new information, connect new material to what they already know, and draw inferences about its significance.
- Good students make sure their study methods are working properly by frequently appraising their own progress.

When low ability and inexperienced students use these skills, they can learn more information and study more efficiently.

PRIOR KNOWLEDGE

When teachers introduce new subject matter, they need to help students grasp its relationship to facts and concepts they have previously learned.

The more students already know about a particular subject, the easier it is for them to acquire new information about it. Teachers can help students learn new information by organizing courses and units of study so that topics build on one another and by helping students focus on relevant background knowledge.

Teachers can also help students grasp relationships between new information and old. Not all students spontaneously relate prior knowledge to new information. For example, a student may not realize that the process involved in solving a particular equation in physics class involves the same process and logic that was used to solve an equation early in the semester.

By identifying central and recurrent patterns in content areas, teachers can help students focus on important information and not get overwhelmed by minor details. For example, teachers can help students learn a new set of scientific theories by helping them early in the learning process to organize the information into patterns and categories. They might include descriptive information about each new theory; historical information telling how the theory emerged; information about the consequences of the theory; information about other theories that explain similar phenomena; and evidence for or against the theory. This process of organizing information helps students to recognize new examples of previously learned concepts and ideas.

As teachers present new information in the classroom, they should ask: "What background knowledge are my students likely to possess that will help them grasp this information?" For example, a child's knowledge of how hot water flows through a pipe can be a helpful analogy in learning and understanding how electricity flows through wires.

HOMEWORK: QUANTITY

Student achievement rises significantly when teachers regularly assign homework and students conscientiously do it.

Extra studying helps children at all levels of ability. One research study reveals that when low ability students do just one to three hours of homework a week, their grades are usually as high as those of average ability students who do not do homework. Similarly, when average ability students do three to five hours of homework a week, their grades usually equal those of high ability students who do no homework.

Homework boosts achievement because the total time spent studying influences how much is learned. Low achieving high school students study less than high achievers and do less homework. Time is not the only ingredient of learning, but without it little can be achieved.

Teachers, parents, and students determine how much, how useful, and how good the homework is. On average, American teachers say they assign about ten hours of homework each week – about two hours per school day. But high school seniors report they spend only four to five hours a week doing homework, and ten percent say they do none at all or have none assigned. In contrast, students in Japan spend about twice as much time studying outside school as American students.

Homework: Quality

Well designed homework assignments relate directly to classwork and extend students' learning beyond the classroom. Homework is most useful when teachers carefully prepare the assignment, thoroughly explain it, and give prompt comments and criticism when the work is completed.

To make the most of what students learn from doing homework, teachers need to give the same care to preparing homework assignments as they give to classroom instruction. When teachers prepare written instructions and discuss homework assignments with students, they find their students take the homework more seriously than if the assignments are simply announced. Students are more willing to do homework when they believe it is useful, when teachers treat it as an integral part of instruction, when it is evaluated by the teacher, and when it counts as a part of the grade.

Assignments that require students to think, and are therefore more interesting, foster their desire to learn both in and out of school. Such activities include explaining what is seen or read in class; comparing, relating, and experimenting with ideas; and analyzing principles.

Effective homework assignments do not just supplement the classroom lesson; they also teach students to be independent learners. Homework gives students experience in following directions, making judgments and comparisons, raising additional questions for study, and developing responsibility and self-discipline.

Assessment

Frequent and systematic monitoring of students' progress helps students, parents, teachers, administrators, and policy makers identify strengths and weaknesses in learning and instruction.

Teachers find out what students already know and what they still need to learn by assessing student work. They use various means, including essays, quizzes and tests, homework, classroom questions, standardized tests, and parents' comments. Teachers can use student errors on tests and in class as early warning signals to point out and correct learning problems before they worsen. Student motivation and achievement improve when teachers provide prompt feedback on assignments.

Students generally take two kinds of tests: classroom tests and standardized tests. Classroom tests help teachers find out if what they are teaching is being learned; thus, these tests serve to evaluate both student and teacher. Standardized tests apply similar gauges to everyone in a specific grade level. By giving standardized tests, school districts can see how achievement progresses over time. Such tests also help schools find out how much of the curriculum is actually being learned. Standardized tests can also reveal problems in the curriculum itself. For example, a recent international mathematics test showed that U.S. students had encountered only 70 percent of what the test covered.

PHONICS

Children get a better start in reading if they are taught phonics. Learning phonics helps them to understand the relationship between letters and sounds and to "break the code" that links the words they hear with the words they see in print.

Until the 1930's and 1940's, most American children learned to read by the phonics method, which stresses the relationships between spoken sounds and printed letters. Children learned the letters of the alphabet and the sounds those letters represent. For several decades thereafter, however, the "look-say" approach to reading was dominant: children were taught to identify whole words in the belief that they would make more rapid progress if they identified whole words at a glance, as adults seem to. Recent research indicates that, on the average, children who are taught phonics get off to a better start in learning to read than children who are not taught phonics.

Identifying words quickly and accurately is one of the cornerstones of skilled reading. Phonics improves the ability of children both to identify words and to sound out new ones. Sounding out the letters in a word is like the first tentative steps of a toddler: it helps children gain a secure verbal footing and expand their vocabularies beyond the limits of basic readers.

Because phonics is a reading tool, it is best taught in the context of reading instruction, not as a separate subject to be mastered. Good phonics strategies include teaching children the sounds of letters in isolation and in words (s/i/t), and how to blend the sounds together (s-s-i-i-t).

Phonics should be taught early but not over-used. If phonics instruction extends for too many years, it can defeat the spirit and excitement of learning to read. Phonics helps children pronounce words approximately, a skill they can learn by the end of second grade. In the meantime, children can learn to put their new phonics skills to work by reading good stories and poems.

Reading Comprehension

Children get more out of a reading assignment when the teacher precedes the lesson with background information and follows it with discussion.

Young readers, and poor readers of every age, do not consistently see connections between what they read and what they already know. When they are given background information about the principal ideas or characters in a story before they read it, they are less apt to become sidetracked or confused and are more likely to understand the story fully. Afterwards, a question and answer discussion session clarifies, reinforces, and extends their understanding.

Good teachers begin the day's reading lesson by preparing children for the story to be read – introducing the new words and concepts they will encounter. Many teachers develop their own introductions or adapt those offered in teachers' manuals.

Such preparation is like a road map: children need it because they may meet new ideas in the story and because they need to be alerted to look for certain special details. Children who are well prepared remember a story's ideas better than those who are not.

In the discussion after the reading lesson, good teachers ask questions that probe the major elements of the story's plot, characters, theme, or moral. ("Why did Pinocchio's nose grow? Why did he lie? What did his father think about his lying? Did their feelings for each other change?") Such questions achieve two purposes: they check students' understanding of what they have just read, and they highlight the kind of meanings and ideas students should look for in future reading selections. These questions also lay the groundwork for later appreciation of the elements of literature such as theme and style. When children take part in a thought provoking discussion of a story, they understand more clearly that the purpose of reading is to get information and insight, not just to decode the words on a page.

STORYTELLING

Telling young children stories can motivate them to read. Storytelling also introduces them to cultural values and literary traditions before they can read, write, and talk about stories by themselves.

Elementary school teachers can introduce young students to the study of literature by telling them fairy tales such as *The Three Billy Goats Gruff* or *Beauty and the Beast* and myths such as *The Iliad*. Even students with low motivation and weak academic skills are more likely to listen, read, write, and work harder in the context of storytelling.

Stories from the oral tradition celebrate heroes who struggle to overcome great obstacles that threaten to defeat them. Children are neither bored nor alienated by learning literature through storytelling; they enjoy, understand, and sympathize naturally with the goats on the bridge, Beauty in a lonely castle, and Hector and Achilles outside the walls of Troy. With the help of skillful questioning, they can also learn to reflect on the deeper meanings of these stories.

Children also benefit from reading stories aloud and from acting out dramatic narrations, whether at home or at school. Parents can begin reading to their children as infants and continue for years to come.

Storytelling can ignite the imaginations of children, giving them a taste of where books can take them. The excitement of storytelling can make reading and learning fun and can instill in children a sense of wonder about life and learning.

Teaching Writing

The most effective way to teach writing is to teach it as a process of brainstorming, composing, revising, and editing.

Students learn to write well through frequent practice. A well-structured assignment has a meaningful topic, a clear sense of purpose, and a real audience. Good writing assignments are often an extension of class reading, discussion, and activities, not isolated exercises.

An effective writing lesson contains these elements:

- *Brainstorming*: Students think and talk about their topics. They collect information and ideas, frequently much more than they will finally use. They sort through their ideas to organize and clarify what they want to say.
- *Composing*: Students compose a first draft. This part is typically time consuming and hard, even for very good writers.
- *Revising*: Students re-read what they have written, sometimes collecting responses from teachers, classmates, parents, and others. The most useful teacher response to an early draft focuses on what students are trying to say, not the mechanics of writing. Teachers can help most by asking for clarification, commenting on vivid expressions or fresh ideas, and suggesting ways to support the main thrust of the writing. Students can then consider the feedback and decide how to use it to improve the next draft.
- *Editing*: Students then need to check their final version for spelling, grammar, punctuation, other writing mechanics, and legibility.

Prompt feedback from teachers on written assignments is important. Students are most likely to write competently when schools routinely require writing in all subject areas, not just in English class.

Vocabulary Instruction

Children learn vocabulary better when the words they study are related to familiar experiences and to knowledge they already possess.

Most children begin school with a sizable speaking and listening comprehension vocabulary. This vocabulary grows as they connect new words to familiar concepts. Teachers can use students' personal experiences and prior knowledge to build vocabulary. Instruction in which children establish relationships among words is more effective than instruction that focuses only on word definitions. This type of vocabulary instruction is an important and specific example of the "Prior Knowledge" finding included below in the Classroom section of this book.

Teachers can foster connections between words by having students group them into categories such that relationships among the words become clear. Children can use their own experiences to create a cluster of synonyms, such as "neat," "tidy," "clean," and "spotless." They can consider similarities and differences in related words, such as "examine" and "scrutinize." They can also group words according to certain features, such as suffixes or prefixes. Encouraging students to talk about personal experiences associated with particular words helps them grasp meanings and relationships among new words and ideas.

Using analogies is another way to help children see the relationship between old and new words. For example, when children are learning the word "province," the analogy "state is to the United States what province is to Canada" relates prior knowledge to a new concept.

READING ALOUD

Hearing good readers read and encouraging students repeatedly to read a passage aloud helps them become good readers.

Helping students learn to read aloud smoothly and easily is an important – but often overlooked – goal of reading instruction. Some authorities have called it the "missing ingredient" in early reading instruction. Teachers can help students become fluent readers by including supported and repeated readings as part of individualized, small group, or classroom instruction.

In supported reading, a child listens to – and reads along with – a good reader. The model can be an adult reader, another student able to read the passage fluently, or a rendition that has been tape recorded. Initially, the student follows along silently or in a soft voice. In subsequent readings of the same passage, the student becomes more fluent and the model gradually fades into the background. In repeated readings, students read a passage over and over until they can read it with ease.

Students may balk at having to read a passage more than once. Teachers can overcome this by providing instructional activities in which repeated readings are a natural component. For example, teachers can have students practice and perform dramatic readings, emphasizing the meaning and emotion of the passage. Teachers can also have students practice reading short stories and poems in unison, and practice singing popular songs together. These types of activities require repeated readings for proficient performance.

Parents can also help improve their children's reading skills by providing opportunities at home for supported and repeated readings.

Purposeful Writing

Students become more interested in writing and the quality of their writing improves when there are significant learning goals for writing assignments and a clear sense of purpose for writing.

Teachers often assign writing tasks to encourage specific types of learning. For example, a teacher may assign a summary if she wants students to identify all the important concepts of a particular topic. Another teacher may assign an analytic essay if he wants students to narrow their focus and examine one aspect in greater depth.

What students learn by writing depends on what they do when they write. Those who simply paraphrase when the assignment calls for analysis may learn facts, but may not be able to draw connections or make inferences about the content. Good teachers identify what they want their writing assignments to accomplish and tell students what those goals are.

Also, students feel the keenest sense of purpose when the audience for their writing extends beyond the teacher. Publishing student writing in school literary magazines and newspapers is one effective way to do this. Students can also write books for the elementary school library, guides to high school life for entering junior high school students, letters, or scripts for school-produced audio and video programs.

Teachers can encourage their students to write for audiences outside of school by having them enter writing contests, write letters to the editors of local newspapers, and correspond with students in other states and countries.

Teachers of all subjects can use writing to help students analyze and understand content. Science teachers, for example, can have students record and organize their ideas about complex concepts in learning logs. History teachers can have students study the life of a turn-of-the-century American immigrant and then interview a present day immigrant; an article comparing the two experiences can be written for the school or local newspaper. A health teacher can have students write about the causes and effects of morphine addiction during the Civil War and relate that information to present day drug problems. Such exercises help students and teachers see more clearly what the student understands – or doesn't yet understand.

Good teachers help students understand that the choices they make in writing affect the quality of their learning in ways that go well beyond the writing itself.

CHILDREN, WHEN READING, CONSTRUCT THEIR OWN MEANING

The meaning constructed from the same text can vary greatly among people because of differences in the knowledge they possess. Sometimes people do not have enough knowledge to understand a text, or they may have knowledge that they do not use fully. Variations in interpretation often arise because people have different conceptions about the topic than the author supposed.

Reading is comprehending, that is, the construction of meaning. Readers construct meaning by interacting with the text on the basis of their existing or prior knowledge about the world. The importance of prior knowledge in reading has been demonstrated through research based on schema theory. According to schema theory, readers understand what they read only as it relates to what they already know. That is, their existing knowledge about a particular topic influences the extent to which they understand what they read about that topic. Because text is not fully explicit, readers must draw from their existing knowledge in order to understand it.

Prior knowledge should be looked at in two ways by the teacher when developing lessons: first, as overall prior knowledge, and second, as specific prior knowledge. Overall prior knowledge is the sum total of learning that students have acquired as a result of their cumulative experiences both in and out of school. Specific prior knowledge is the particular information a student needs in order to understand text that deals with a certain topic. Specific prior knowledge is of two types: text-specific knowledge calls for understanding about the type of text – for example, a story has a beginning, a middle, and an end; topic-specific knowledge entails understanding something about the topic – for example, knowing about dinosaurs before reading a book on pre-historic animals.

Overall prior knowledge is expanded continually by a variety of means which include extensive reading and writing. The more students read and write, the more their prior knowledge grows which, in turn, strengthens their ability to construct meaning as they read.

Teachers must not only recognize that independent reading and writing activities are crucial for expanding students' prior knowledge. They must also systematically include such activities in their literacy program. In addition, both text-specific and topic-specific prior knowledge play an important role in helping students construct meaning. Activating only students' topical prior knowledge without helping them to consider the actual structure of the text does not improve their meaning-making abilities. Conversely, teachers can effectively improve these abilities when they activate all levels of students' prior knowledge appropriately.

Effective reading instruction can develop engaged readers who are knowledgeable, strategic, motivated, and socially interactive

The National Reading Research Center's over-arching goal is to study how to cultivate highly engaged, self-determining readers who are the architects of their own learning. A unifying theme running throughout our research is that students will acquire the competencies and motivations to read for diverse aesthetic and academic purposes, such as gaining knowledge, interpreting an author's perspective, escaping into the literary world, performing a task, sharing reactions to stories and informational texts, or taking social and political action in response to what is read.

Until recently, reading instruction focused almost exclusively on cognitive aspects – for example, the mechanics of reading. However, teaching students to become literate involves much more. Literacy depends on a myriad of factors related to the *context* of literacy activities (for example, the kind of social interaction that takes place during a reading group discussion) and the child's *personal attributes*, including cognitive development. An engaged reader: 1) uses prior knowledge to gain information from new material; 2) uses a variety of skills in a strategic way to gain information independently; 3) is internally motivated to read for information and for pleasure; and 4) interacts socially to make gains in literacy development.

The context of literacy instruction and personal attributes, in addition to cognitive development, influence children's reading success in profound ways. Therefore, when planning instruction, teachers must make provisions in daily lessons for factors such as students' motivation to read. For example, choosing to read is an important ingredient of engaged reading. It has been found that allowing students to choose reading material of interest to them is a powerful motivator that fosters independent reading habits. Effective teachers make use of this knowledge on a regular basis in planning and executing instruction.

Engaged reading, wherein students construct their own knowledge, is a form of engaged learning. Engaged reading goes beyond a reader's interaction with text. It is a means by which one becomes a member of a community of readers and society at large. To be engaged readers, students must recognize the value of reading and their own potential as readers and learners. Teachers can help students develop this recognition by providing them with access to multiple sources of reading and resources for learning.

Engaged reading develops in literacy classrooms where self and mutual assessment are as routine as they are in everyday life. These assessments which promote engaged reading take a variety of forms, including: the constant, strategic monitoring of one's progress while reading (for example, meta-cognition); the comparing of one's opinions and reactions to what one has read with those of others; and the monitoring of other people's reactions to one's own constructions of meaning. When such processes become regular events during literacy instruction, assessment and literacy learning become intertwined, such that learning is supported at the same time that it is assessed.

PHONEMIC AWARENESS, A PRECURSOR TO COMPETENCY IN IDENTIFY-
ING WORDS, IS ONE OF THE BEST PREDICTORS OF LATER SUCCESS IN
READING

*Children's awareness of the phonemic structure of spoken words is an
extremely strong predictor of their success in learning to read. Because
useful knowledge of spelling/sound correspondences depends on such
phonemic awareness, children who fail to acquire it are severely handicapped in their ability to master print.*

Phonemic awareness – discerning that spoken language is com-
posed of phonemes – is an important predictor of success in learning
to read. It involves a child's ability to hear the sounds in a word and to
distinguish between words based on the different sounds. Phonemic
awareness helps children learn the letter-sound correspondences
needed to read and spell words. Studies have shown that phonemic
awareness training improves children's ability to read and spell.
Unless word identification is effortless and automatic, the reader cannot devote attention to constructing meaning while reading.

Phonics – instruction in the relationship between letters and
sounds – can help children attain automatic, visual recognition of
spelling patterns within words for word recognition. Efficient recognition of spelling patterns, in turn, depends on accurate and automatic recognition of individual letters. Studies of young children
show that the most important precursor to success in learning to read
is rapid recognition of the letters of the alphabet. Studies also show
that the efficient use of sound patterns in speech depends on the
awareness of phonemes in spoken language. This awareness relates
strongly to success in beginning reading. Many children develop these
prerequisites without formal instruction. This is likely due both to the
frequency and quality of early experiences these children have with
oral language and to the amount of exposure they have to print before
entering school.

Effective beginning reading instruction is that which contains a
balance of activities designed to improve word recognition, including

phonics instruction and reading meaningful text. Writing and spelling activities are also part of effective reading instruction because they affect overall reading ability in a positive way. Encouraging children to make invented spellings (to spell words as they sound) helps develop phonemic awareness as well as increases knowledge of spelling patterns. Effective teachers interweave these activities within their instruction and, above all, ensure that phonics teaching is not done apart from connected, informative, engaging text.

MODELING IS AN IMPORTANT FORM OF CLASSROOM SUPPORT FOR
LITERACY LEARNING

Strategies for approaching different types of reading have different types of purposes. Teachers should not leave their students to discover these strategies on their own, because most of them won't. Rather, teachers should forthrightly show them. For example, a teacher can effectively model out loud for students the way to determine the main idea or most important point of a text. The teacher can also model reading itself, not only during read-alouds with the children, but also by reading themselves during Sustained Silent Reading time. Just as with sustained writing time, sustained silent reading is a time during which everyone is involved, including the teacher.

In the literacy classroom, learning is a constructive, interactive process. As children develop literacy skills, they need careful guidance and support within their reading, writing, listening, and speaking experiences during instruction. Support in this context is sometimes referred to as scaffolding. Teacher modeling, a form of scaffolding, is a way of showing students how to approach a task such as finding the main idea of a story.

There are two types of modeling: implicit and explicit. Implicit modeling occurs as part of the literacy experience – for example, reading a fable aloud to children while also engaging them in the meaning of the story and conveying a purpose for reading. Explicit modeling entails demonstrating to students how to approach a task – such as how to use a table of contents.

Two types of explicit modeling are talk-alouds and think-alouds. In a talk-aloud activity, the teacher gives students a series of steps they must follow to complete a task, and then asks questions to guide students through the task from beginning to end. In a think-aloud activity, the teacher shares with students the thinking process one must go through to approach a task and complete it. On the one hand, in the talk-aloud method, the teacher's emphasis is on the procedural steps used to complete a task like finding the main idea. On the other hand, in the think-aloud approach, the teacher's emphasis is on the actual thinking process that he or she goes through in approaching and carrying out a cognitive task like inferring a main idea.

Both forms of modeling, implicit and explicit, have a place in the well-balanced literacy program. They are designed to show students strategies they can use on their own to gain an understanding of new material. It is critical, however, that modeling practices be seated within whole literacy events because they easily become instances of isolated-skills teaching. Ensuring that modeling practices take place within an appropriate instructional context requires continuous vigilance from the teacher.

Storybook reading, done in the context of sharing experiences, ideas, and opinions, is a highly demanding mental activity for children

Shared reading is defined as any rewarding reading situation in which a learner – or group of learners – sees the text, observes an expert (usually the teacher) reading it with fluency and expression, and is invited to read along. The learner is in the role of receiving support, and the teacher-expert accepts and encourages all efforts and approximations the learner makes. Each reading situation is a relaxed, social one, with emphasis on enjoyment and appreciation of the stories, songs, rhymes, chants, raps, and poems. The literature is carefully chosen for its high quality of language and illustrations and often includes re-readings of favorite stories and poems. Following shared reading, students have opportunities to re-read the literature independently.

Storybook reading is most effective for developing children's ability to understand stories when it involves far more than reading aloud the words of an author. Readers construct meaning about what they read using their background or prior knowledge. Moreover, readers construct meaning as they interact with peers and adults in discussing stories. Similarly, the discussion among readers and listeners that occurs in response to shared text is an important part of the story-time experience. Using interactive strategies such as story-based discussions along with storybook reading helps children construct meaning and understand stories that are read to them.

Recent research indicates that it is important to provide children with daily positive experiences involving stories and other literature. Opportunities for such experiences include reading and retelling stories, discussing stories critically, role-playing, responding to stories both orally and in writing or through expressive art (for example, drawing projects), and sharing books with peers. Children support one another in their efforts to understand and reflect on stories. When children participate in one-to-one read aloud events, the quality and complexity of their responses increase. Also, when children have repeated experiences with stories, their interpretive responses become more varied and more complex.

Children's stories, both oral and written, have been the subject of important research on the development of children's ability to construct coherent text. As children hear stories told and read, they learn the structure as well as the linguistic features of stories or narrative text. Children often display this knowledge by "talking like a book" when they pretend to read their favorite stories. There is ample research evidence to show that teachers who read aloud to children foster their ability to deal effectively with the narrative text of the stories. Children are engaging in their most intellectually demanding work when they share ideas and opinions about stories, and share experiences related to stories read or told to them.

Responding to literature helps students construct their
own meaning which may not always be the same for all readers

*Classrooms where responses to literature thrive seem to be characterized
by teachers' valuing of responses as the crux of literacy growth. Valuing
of response in the classroom is evident when teachers (A) provide
opportunities for response, (B) provide response models, and (C) receive
children's responses in all their diversity.*

Responding is a natural part of the reading process. When students read a piece of literature they respond to it by using their prior
knowledge to construct meaning. That is, their transaction with the
text results in the construction of their own personal meaning.
Responding helps students develop their meta-cognitive skills which
are important to constructing meaning. Students develop these self-
monitoring skills by being encouraged continuously to think about
and respond to what they read and write.

Reading informational text is different from reading literature
such as fiction or poetry. One reads informational material to find
factual information that serves a specific purpose. With fiction or
poetry, the reader's aim is primarily aesthetic. for example, to become
engrossed by an intriguing plot or clutched by an emotion evoking
description of nature. Teachers honor the difference between informational text and literature when they allow students to read a selec-
tion of fiction or poetry without asking them to find facts. Permitting
students to read fiction and poetry aesthetically enhances the goal of
providing children with pleasurable experiences with literature.

There is a commonly accepted response which is expected from
students, and there is a more personal response which differs from
student to student for any given piece of literature. And within the
bounds of commonly accepted responses, there are often a variety of
interpretations. Teachers must be prepared to expect, respect, and
accept a variety of student responses and accommodate them within
their literacy instruction. Students' personal responses can be

expressed through a variety of means such as oral discussion, debate, role-playing, and graphic illustration. Encouraging students' personal responses to literature improves their ability to construct meaning. Over time, students develop more and more complex responses to literature that help them become better at constructing meaning.

Children who are schooled in response-centered classrooms where their responses to literature are valued, develop a sense of ownership, pride, and respect with regard to learning. Out of this shared value of learning comes a sense of community, which in turn bolsters everyone's efforts – those of students and teachers alike.

CHILDREN WHO ENGAGE IN DAILY DISCUSSIONS ABOUT WHAT THEY READ ARE MORE LIKELY TO BECOME CRITICAL READERS AND LEARNERS

"I, too, have learned many things about talk from my work in the classroom and from examining the talk of students. This research has informed my practice; I can never again hold a monopoly on talk in the classroom as did the teachers of my educational experience. My voice is one among the many teachers, many students, many learners in the room. We are creating a new legacy, one of voice, empowerment, and interaction. Through our talk, we get together, get along, and get to the business of teaching and learning."

–M.A. Cintorino

Students' discussion in classrooms is important to their learning. Research shows that students' verbal exchanges about content improve learning and increase their level of thinking. The social nature of learning implies that, because each context is different, participants must always evaluate what to say, when and how, consider options, and make choices. Learning rests on taking these actions.

Using discussion to connect literature and other texts with a variety of experiences and the prior knowledge of the reader maximizes students' learning, given that they critically discuss topics worth talking about. This interactive approach is based on the knowledge that, on the one hand, simply acquiring information like names and dates does not amount to significant learning. On the other hand, discussion among students, at any age, in which they hear different points of view and collaborate to solve problems, serves as a catalyst for the development of logical reasoning skills.

Traditionally, discussion in classrooms has not been common. As students advance through the grades, opportunities for discussion in the classroom appear to decrease. This situation has been so prevalent that in one study of secondary English classes, the researcher called discussion the "forgotten language art." Nevertheless, when students are given opportunities to talk and listen, they can and do converse in productive ways to learn in all areas of the curriculum. Questions, rethinking, and refined understandings result when students discuss their understandings of themes or concepts that appear in text.

Given the importance of discussion for effective learning, effective teaching involves providing students with ample opportunities to engage in daily discussions with one another. Small group and peer-to-peer interaction are valuable in promoting academic and social learning. Children who rely on each other for help learn more than children who work alone. Instruction can be organized in a variety of ways to facilitate discussion. One way is to form a cooperative learning group of students with varying abilities to read, discuss, or respond to a piece of text. Another way is to pair students with a "buddy" to interact and problem solve. The more students work in groups or pairs, the more productive their discussions will become, especially as their social skills become more refined.

Expert readers have strategies that they use to construct meaning before, during and after reading

One of the hallmarks of education and literacy is the ability to read thoughtfully and flexibly. The development of strategic reading is a life-long endeavor that is supported by parents, peers, and teachers who instill enthusiasm, knowledge, and confidence in students. As students learn to regulate their own reading and to use strategies for different purposes, they become independent learners who read with confidence and enjoyment. Thus, strategic reading contributes directly to lifelong education and personal satisfaction.

As students become proficient readers, they develop a set of plans or strategies for solving problems they encounter in their reading experiences. Much research has been conducted to identify these strategies. Although much remains to be done in this area of literacy research, at least five important strategies have been identified as critical to learning and therefore should be taught in a good literacy program.

- *Inferencing* is the process of reaching conclusions based on information within the text and is the cornerstone of constructing meaning. Inferencing includes making predictions using prior knowledge combined with information available from text.
- *Identifying important information* is the process of finding critical facts and details in narrative (stories) or expository (informational) text. The task of identifying important information in narrative text differs from that of identifying important information in expository text because the structures of the text are different. However, students can be taught strategies for approaching each type of text.
- *Monitoring* is a meta-cognitive or self-awareness process that expert constructors of meaning use to help themselves overcome problems as they read. For example, when good readers have difficulty understanding a paragraph, they become aware of the problem and stop immediately to "fix" it by employing a strategy such as re-reading.
- *Summarizing* is a process that involves pulling together important

information gathered from a long passage of text.

- *Question generating* involves readers asking themselves questions they want answered from reading that require them to integrate information while they read.

These five strategies for constructing meaning are based on substantial research. Many studies in which non-expert readers were trained to use these strategies have shown very promising results. Effective teachers incorporate these strategies into their on-going literacy instruction. When modeling these strategies, they treat them as a set of devices for constructing meaning instead of as independent activities that are isolated from the literacy context.

Children's reading and writing abilities develop together

Historical and cross-cultural evidence suggests that literacy in a society might entail reading and writing as separate or related entities. We believe strongly that in our society, at this point in history, reading and writing, to be understood and appreciated fully, should be viewed together, learned together, and used together.

Both reading and writing are constructive processes. A similar, if not the same, level of intellectual activity underlies both reading and writing: interactions between the reader/writer and text lead to new knowledge and interpretations of text. Just as thoughtful readers read for a specific purpose by activating prior knowledge about the topic at hand, writers activate prior knowledge that relates to the topic and have a purpose for writing – to impart meaning to a reader.

While reading, readers re-read and modify meaning accordingly. While writing, writers think about the topic and the more they think, the better developed their writing becomes. They also think about what they've written, re-read it, and make revisions to improve it. Lastly, readers finalize the meaning they have constructed so far. Writers do likewise; they settle on their final composition.

The processes of reading and writing not only unfold in similar ways, they tend to be used together. This is natural because in every-day life reading and writing frequently occur together. For example, a person receives a letter – via the postal service or electronic mail – reads it, then answers it in writing, perhaps re-reading portions of the letter while constructing the response. Moreover, learning about reading and writing takes place in a social context that contains written language and where people use and talk about written language.

When reading and writing are taught together the benefits are greater than when they are taught separately. Research has begun to show that writing leads to improved reading achievement, reading leads to better writing performance, and combined instruction leads to improvements in both areas. Moreover, research has shown that engaging learners in the greater variety of experiences provided when reading and writing instruction are combined leads to a higher level of thinking than when either process is taught alone. Since thinking is a critical part of meaning construction, students will become better thinkers if they are taught in classrooms where meaning is actively constructed through reading and writing. Teachers can be most effective in helping students to become better readers, writers, and thinkers when they weave integrated reading and writing activities into their literacy instruction.

THE MOST VALUABLE FORM OF READING ASSESSMENT REFLECTS OUR
CURRENT UNDERSTANDING ABOUT THE READING PROCESS AND SIMU-
LATES AUTHENTIC READING TASKS

*The optimist says assessment will drive instruction in the future and
new and better assessments are being developed to do the job. But the
cautious optimist says this will only happen if educators at all levels
understand the difference between sound and unsound assessment and
can integrate sound assessments into the instruction process in effective
ways.*

Until very recently reading assessment focused on measuring students' performance on a hierarchy of isolated skills that, when put
together, were thought to compose "reading." Now it is known that
the whole act of reading is greater than the sum of its parts or isolated skills. Moreover, these parts are interrelated within a literacy context and do not always develop in a hierarchical way. The discrete
skills concept has been replaced with the current constructive, interactive view on literacy learning. This perspective grew out of recent
research on cognition that revolutionized what we know about learning. However, by and large, practices in literacy assessment have not
kept pace with what is known about literacy learning, although they
are beginning to change.

The role of standardized tests in the literacy program is likely to
remain important. Because state and local school districts are likely to
continue using norm-referenced, standardized tests to evaluate literacy programs, State tests and the National Assessment of Educational
Progress (NAEP) are undergoing substantial changes. The majority of
these changes involve creating authentic assessments – appraisals that
account for critical aspects of reading and that parallel everyday reading tasks. Changes that are moving assessment closer to simulating
authentic reading tasks include: using unabridged text directly from
the original source for assessing meaning construction; accounting
for students' prior knowledge before reading; incorporating samples
(portfolios) of student work; and making student self-assessment part

of the standardized testing program.

Literacy assessments done in the classroom that involve performance tasks are beginning to provide valuable information needed to direct instructional decision making. Many teachers are turning to portfolio assessments that include multiple measures taken over time of individual students' reading and writing. Well constructed portfolios contain samples of student work, including representative pieces of work-in-progress and exceptional pieces, students' reflection about their work, and evaluation criteria. For example, pieces of students' writing in which they share their thinking and feeling about their reading – text analyses from their own point of view – may be included in portfolios. Creating and using performance assessments as alternatives and/or supplements to norm-referenced tests are helping to transform reading instruction and learning in today's state-of-the-art classroom.

Learning Mathematics

Children in early grades learn mathematics more effectively when they use physical objects in their lessons.

Numerous studies of mathematics achievement at different grade and ability levels show that children benefit when real objects are used as aids in learning mathematics. Teachers call these objects "manipulatives."

Objects that students can look at and hold are particularly important in the early stages of learning a math concept because they help the student understand by visualizing. Students can tie later work to these concrete activities.

The type or design of the objects used is not particularly important; they can be blocks, marbles, poker chips, cardboard cutouts – almost anything. Students do as well with inexpensive or homemade materials as with costly, commercial versions.

The cognitive development of children and their ability to understand ordinarily move from the concrete to the abstract. Learning from real objects takes advantage of this fact and provides a firm foundation for the later development of skills and concepts.

ALL STUDENTS CAN AND MUST LEARN MATHEMATICS, WHICH SHOULD SERVE AS A "PUMP," NOT A "FILTER"

Myth: Learning mathematics requires special ability, which most students do not have.

Reality: Only in the United States do people believe that learning mathematics depends on special ability. In other countries, students, parents, and teachers all expect that most students can master mathematics if only they work hard enough. The record of accomplishment in these countries – and in some intervention programs in the United States – shows that most students can learn much more mathematics than is commonly assumed in this country.

The idea that all students can and must learn mathematics means that the study of mathematics, by serving as a pump – an access to success – can transform the learning of the general population. All students must have the opportunity to learn mathematics.

In the past it was assumed that problem solving ability was tied to the ability to perform paper-and-pencil calculations. Years of teachers' and students' time were spent trying to remediate children who lacked this ability. The emphasis on remediation was based on the premise that mathematics is linear and hierarchical and must be taught in a prescribed order – rote skills first, problem solving later. But research shows that repeating the same uninteresting tasks in the same unimaginative way is not effective. Students learn best when they are intellectually challenged so that they are motivated to fill in mathematical gaps when necessary. The teacher's role is to provide stimulating problems and environment to motivate mathematical learning. In fact, research points out that certain teaching strategies can help all students develop "mathematical power." Providing students with real-life problems to investigate is just one strategy for helping them develop an understanding of the mathematical concepts that underlie a variety of problems.

Tracking, on the other hand, when it is used to filter students out of mathematics, is antithetical to the development of mathematical power. Little learning is expected of students in lower tracks and, as a result, they produce little and lose the opportunity to work in mathematics related occupations. Teachers of these tracks often feel like second-class citizens too and lose their enthusiasm and creativity over the years. Tracking fosters an elitism that contributes to the under representation of women and non-Asian minorities in mathematics fields and careers that rely on a solid mathematics background. And, tracking is a poor substitute for implementing a wide variety of the enrichment activities at the pre-high school level and of mathematics courses at the high school level, including advanced placement courses, that can stimulate the quickest students to greater achievement.

All school mathematics courses should be of high quality and challenge all students to high achievement. Parents and students must be shown that achievement in mathematics does not depend on an accident of birth such as innate talent, but that it is attainable through hard work – the same way all skills are successfully accessed.

TEACHERS NEED TO LISTEN TO STUDENTS AND TO INCORPORATE INTO THEIR INSTRUCTION WHAT THEY LEARN FROM LISTENING

"The first several years of teaching I really was into 'This is the section of the book that we're doing today, and here's the practice problems, and now we'll go over homework, and then I'll teach you how to do it, then you'll practice, and then you'll have some to try before you go home,' and that kind of thing. I teach very differently now."

Teachers who listen to students, and who plan instruction based on what they learn from listening, transform student learning. For example, two children may arrive at the same solution to a problem but with different strategies. These strategies may reflect different levels of understanding and suggest different follow-up activities. Moreover, teachers who listen carefully to students' mathematical explanations often find that their students know a great deal of mathematics at an informal level. By building upon this informal knowledge, teachers can help their students construct more sophisticated concepts.

Effective teachers listen carefully to how students go about solving problems. They know their students' mathematical strengths and weaknesses and they can develop a teaching strategy based on this understanding. Research shows that when teachers act upon their knowledge of student thinking, their beliefs about learning and instruction, their classroom practices and, most importantly, their students' learning and beliefs can be affected profoundly.

Students learn mathematics best when they construct their own mathematical understanding

One of the most difficult shifts for teachers is to relinquish their role of keeper of "the right answer."

Students who construct their own mathematical understanding transform their mathematical potential. It takes courage to begin using the *constructivist* approach in the classroom, but the rewards can be great. Teachers often start with an experiment – a somewhat ill-defined but interesting mathematical problem or application for students to solve. They resist pleas to solve the problem for their students. They often find that their best students resist the change in teaching and learning at first. After all, the best students have succeeded in the old mode, even if they found the mathematics boring. The teachers give the experiment time to succeed.

As students grapple with constructing their own knowledge, they may ask questions that the teacher cannot answer. They may go down mathematical paths that their teacher has not trod. They may devise algorithms that are unknown to their teacher. Teachers too need to construct their own mathematical and pedagogical knowledge. As teachers become learners they model the mathematical behavior they expect of their students.

Teachers must assume a new role if students are to construct their own mathematical understanding. Rather than just being the information givers – pouring mathematical knowledge into the student's head, teachers must provide stimulating mathematical problem situations that encourage mathematical learning. Students must change from being passive recipients to becoming active seekers of knowledge. Students must also learn to verify their own mathematical knowledge.

STUDENTS NEED TO LEARN MORE AND DIFFERENT TYPES OF MATHEMATICS

It is now possible to execute almost all of the mathematical techniques taught from kindergarten through the first two years of college on hand-held calculators.

The need for a work force equipped with more and different mathematical concepts is transforming the mathematics curriculum. Non-routine problems rarely involve ideas from just one part of mathematics. Just as the printing press made calligraphy obsolete as a common writing tool while, at the same time, it increased the need for people to read and write. So too technology is making pen and pencil calculations obsolete while, at the same time, increasing the need for people to model and solve complex problems. Thus the curriculum at all grade levels needs to include geometry and measurement, probability and statistics, pre-algebra or algebra, patterns, relations, functions, and discrete mathematics.

This suggested curricular reform is not as radical as it first appears. Many countries have used an integrated curriculum successfully for years, and teachers across the United States have already begun to develop instructional units based on problem situations that involve a variety of mathematical content areas and that may take a number of weeks for the students to investigate.

Some teachers worry that teaching more and different types of mathematics will crowd the mathematics curriculum. Constructing one's own mathematical understanding and solving complex mathematical problems and applications are very time consuming. It may not be possible to cover the same ground using this approach as one would using the lecture method. Yet research indicates that the mathematical understanding students construct themselves is deep and enduring – that students taught this way can score as well as their peers on low-level mathematics skill items and better on problem solving and conceptual items. Orchestrating the major mathematical concepts that students should understand and eliminating from deep coverage those items of less importance are difficult new roles for teachers.

MATHEMATICAL DISCUSSION SHOULD BE A DAILY PART OF CLASS-
ROOM ACTIVITY

If a child asks you if this answer is right, and you say "yes," you've robbed him of the real learning. It's a question of when you say "good," not if you say it. Once you've probed for understanding, and you're sure that the child knows, then to say, "You've convinced me, that's terrific, what you said really made sense to me. Why don't you share it with the rest of the class?"

Mathematical discourse transforms student learning. In offering praise too quickly teachers sometimes lose the opportunity for productive mathematical discussions, a key ingredient for building mathematical power. The lecture mode of instruction also discourages mathematical discourse in the classroom. Recent research shows that classrooms where students engage in a rich mathematical dialog with their peers as well as with their teachers are effective learning environments. Students need to be actively involved in questioning, conjecturing, defining, and explaining.

Teachers can shape the classroom environment to encourage mathematical discussion. They can encourage the participation of all students by valuing each student's contribution, by reducing the risk of ridicule for being wrong, by encouraging honest disagreement, and by making sure that all students are included in the discussion. Mathematical discussion that is rigorous but open minded should be a regular and valued part of classroom activity.

When teachers openly discuss their own mathematical thinking and demonstrate the process by which they solved a problem, they encourage this active mathematical behavior in their students. Teachers cannot expect students to tackle difficult mathematical problems, to discuss, question, define, and conjecture if they do not do so themselves. They cannot expect students to be curious and excited about mathematics unless they are.

TEACHERS NEED TO BECOME "INFORMED GUIDES" TO THE LEARNER

How to get and maintain all the students' engagement? How to make sense of what the students are thinking? How to help them move toward appropriate and connected understandings of fractions or other concepts? From moment to moment, you have to consider whether to praise, explain, solicit others' ideas, let an issue grow, or even stir up trouble in order to press on a crucial mathematical point. Day after day in the classroom, students say things you have never considered. Day after day they have trouble with ideas you used to think were simple. And day after day, they catch you off guard with what captures their interest and what they reach for.

Teachers who "guide" rather than "tell" transform student learning. The role of informed guide is much more difficult to assume than that of the lecturer. As teachers focus more on guiding their students' learning they need to know more mathematics. According to the Mathematical Association of America's *A CALL FOR CHANGE;*

- Teachers need to recognize the relationship between what they teach and what is taught at other levels of school mathematics. They need, for example, to understand the close parallel among the development of integer arithmetic in the elementary grades, the algebra of polynomials in the middle and early high school curriculum, and the ideas of number systems explored later in high school. They should explore the relationships between geometry and algebra and the use of one to investigate the other.

- Case studies indicate that teachers who have a good background in mathematics also add a richness to their lessons, involve students extensively in mathematical dialog, and capitalize on students' questions and discussions to weave and extend mathematical relationships. Such teachers guide their students to discover mathematical concepts and procedures. They do not list definitions and step-by-step procedures for students to memorize without understanding their meaning and function. Research indicates that classroom behavior is affected by an interplay among teachers' general and content-specific knowledge of mathematics, their understanding of how children think about mathematics, and their beliefs about mathematics and about how children learn it.

SOLVING WORD PROBLEMS

Students will become more adept at solving math problems if teachers encourage them to think through a problem before they begin working on it, guide them through the thinking process, and give them regular and frequent practice in solving problems.

Good mathematical problem solvers usually analyze the challenges they face and explore alternative strategies before starting work. Unsuccessful problem solvers often act impulsively when given a problem and follow the first idea that occurs to them. Too often, school instruction emphasizes and rewards the rapid solving of problems and fails to recognize and reinforce thoughtful behavior.

For example, consider the following elementary level word problem: "Susan wants to buy a candy bar that costs 30 cents. The machine will take nickels, dimes and quarters in any combination. List the different combinations of coins Susan could use to pay for her candy."

A good teacher will first ask questions to ensure that the students understand the problem, such as which coins does the machine take? Can all the coins be the same? Do you think there is more than one answer for the problem? The teacher might also encourage students to formulate their own questions or retell the problem in their own words. Students can suggest strategies to solve the problem, such as making a chart or list of different combinations of coins that could be used.

After different strategies are identified, students can begin to solve the problem. If a plan does not work, the teacher can ask additional questions or provide hints to help students formulate other approaches. After the problem is solved, the teacher can have students analyze their strategies and consider alternatives.

Frequent practice in solving problems is most effective when teachers ask students questions about their thinking, give them hints when they are stumped, and help them see how some problems are related. These practices help students learn how to think problems through for themselves. They can also be taught other techniques to help them correctly solve problems, such as adding a diagram, removing extraneous information, and reorganizaing data.

CALCULATORS, COMPUTERS, AND RELATED TECHNOLOGY CAN BE
EFFECTIVE TOOLS IN THE TEACHING AND LEARNING OF MATHEMAT-
ICS

Failure to introduce and to use calculators and computers in school cre-
ates a needless barrier between what is happening in students' everyday
lives and what they are being taught in school. For mathematics educa-
tion to remain viable in the future, it must include a major role for the
computer now.

Calculators, computers, and related technology used as tools in
the teaching and learning of mathematics transform the learner from
calculator to critical thinker. Technology implies a shift from using
brain power for computational tasks to using brain power to think
critically, to communicate clearly, to solve mathematical problems,
and to apply mathematics to complex scientific and social problems.
Research shows that the proper use of calculators and computers can
in fact enhance mathematics learning at all stages. Calculators and
computers can take the drudgery out of mathematics by handling
routine arithmetic and algebraic calculations, freeing the learner to
concentrate on the problem that requires such calculations.
Calculators and computers can be used to illustrate mathematical
concepts graphically and this kind of visual representation can help
understanding. Computers can simulate a variety of modeling
options, freeing the learner to determine the most appropriate model
to use in a given application.

The continual development of new technology – graphing calculators; computer based exploratory tools such as spreadsheets, LOGO,
the Geometric Supposer, and the Geometers' Sketch Pad; and hyper-
media – requires teachers to continually enhance their technological
skills. Professional mathematics and computer science education
journals and in-service workshops can help provide this enhancement
for more effective mathematics teaching and learning.

Science Experiments

Children learn science best when they are able to do experiments, so they can witness "science in action."

Reading about scientific principles or having a teacher explain them is frequently not enough. Cause and effect are not always obvious, and it may take an experiment to make that clear. Experiments help children actually see how the natural world works.

Scientific explanations sometimes conflict with the way students may suppose that things happen or work. For example, most students would probably think that a basketball will fall faster than a ping-pong ball because the basketball is larger and heavier. Unless a teacher corrects this intuitive assumption by having the students perform an experiment and see the results, the students will continue to trust their intuition, even though the textbook or the teacher tells them the effect of gravity on both objects is exactly the same and that both will reach the floor at the same instant.

Many students have misconceptions even after taking a science course because they have not had opportunities to test and witness the evidence that would change their minds. To clear up misconceptions, students need to be given the chance to predict the results they anticipate in an experiment. For example, the mistaken idea that the basketball will fall faster than the ping-pong ball can be tested experimentally. The teacher can then explain why the original hypothesis was faulty. In this way experiments help students use the scientific method to distinguish facts from opinions and misconceptions.

Estimating

Although students need to learn how to find exact answers to arithmetic problems, good math students also learn the helpful skill of estimating answers. This skill can be taught.

Many people can tell almost immediately when a total seems right or wrong. They may not realize it, but they are using a math skill called estimating. Estimating can also be valuable to children learning math.

When students can make good estimates of the answer to an arithmetic problem, it shows they understand the problem. This skill leads them to reject unreasonable answers and to know whether they are "in the ballpark."

Research has identified three key steps used by good estimators; these can be taught to all students:

• Good estimators begin by altering numbers to more manageable forms – by rounding, for example.

• They change parts of a problem into forms they can handle more easily. In a problem with several steps, they may rearrange the steps to make estimation easier.

• They also adjust two numbers at a time when making their estimates. Rounding one number higher and one number lower is an example of this technique.

Before students can become good at estimating, they need to have quick, accurate recall of basic facts. They also need a good grasp of the place-value system (ones, tens, hundreds, etc.).

Estimating is a practical skill; for example, it comes in very handy when shopping. It can also help students in many areas of mathematics and science that they will study in the future.

STUDENTS NEED SHARED LEARNING EXPERIENCES

Research indicates several positive effects of cooperative learning in mathematics education.

Cooperative learning transforms the teaching and learning of mathematics to model the work force environment. In the work force, teams of people collaborate to solve difficult problems. The expertise of each team member adds a dimension to the solution process. Students need to learn to work cooperatively, too. Students working together help each other learn. Together, students can often tackle challenging situations that would be beyond the capacities of the individuals who comprise the group. The group situation can motivate students and stimulate mathematical discussion, thus helping each student realize her or his own potential.

In order for this group process to work effectively, the teacher must carefully prepare the learning environment. Problems presented to the group should be too difficult or too complex for one child to solve alone. The problems should also pique the group's interest and curiosity. The teacher must ensure that all children participate in the group work and learn cooperative skills. Teachers themselves may need in-service education in using cooperative learning strategies so they can successfully implement them in the classroom.

When cooperative learning is coupled with individual accountability, cooperative learning leads to greater academic achievement. Cooperative learning also can increase the self-esteem and self-confidence of the learners and lead to positive intergroup relations – including cross racial and cross cultural friendships and social acceptance of main streamed children – and greater ability to use social skills.

CURRICULAR AND PEDAGOGICAL CHANGE IN MATHEMATICS CANNOT OCCUR WITHOUT ACCOMPANYING CHANGE IN STUDENT ASSESSMENT

Through assessment, a better understanding should be obtained of how students are relating mathematical ideas to each other and if they are building an integrated notion of mathematics. Making sure that assessment is integral to instruction should mean that the information obtained is directly useful for guiding instruction. In short, good assessment is good instruction.

Curricular and pedagogical changes in mathematics must transform how students are assessed. As mathematics curricula and pedagogy are changed, the instruments for measuring student achievement must also be changed. It is not fair to students, teachers, or school districts to be measured by outdated standards.

The majority of standardized tests our children take are still overly reliant on multiple choice items that measure predominantly low level mathematics skills. Although they are beginning to reflect the changes in mathematics teaching and learning, these tests include few types of questions that require higher order problem solving skills. School districts should analyze standardized tests and use the test that most closely assesses meaningful standards that are in place, such as the NCTM standards.

Researchers are developing alternative assessment tools that both measure student achievement and promote learning. Performance assessment, student interviews, group project reports, and portfolios are a few in the wide range of new assessment tools that researchers are investigating and teachers are beginning to use.

Lasting change takes broad support

It costs State legislators and bureaucrats relatively little to fashion a new instructional policy that calls for novel sorts of classroom work. These officials can easily ignore the pedagogical past, for they do not work in classrooms, and they bear little direct responsibility for what is done in localities – even if it is done partly at their insistence. However, teachers and students cannot ignore the pedagogical past, because it is their past. If instructional changes are to be made, they must make them. Teachers construct their practices gradually, out of their experience as students, their professional education, and their previous encounters with policies designed to change their practice. Teaching is less a set of garments that can be changed at will than a way of knowing, of seeing, and of being.

Broad support from the educational community is needed to advance the reform effort and transform it to state-of-the-art. Teachers willing to risk making the recommended shifts in classroom practices are at the forefront of the reform in teaching and learning mathematics. Yet systematic change cannot occur unless the members of the learning team – students, parents, school administrators, and policy makers – are also key participants in the process. Past reform efforts have died out because the whole learning team was not involved. The rationale for changing mathematics teaching and learning, and plans for implementing the changes, should be disseminated to all of these groups. The learning team needs to be involved in the construction of the new school mathematics environment.

Although research on the current reform movement in mathematics is on-going and as yet incomplete, several components of the reform's success have emerged. It is evident that teachers cannot accomplish it alone. A coordinated school-based reform effort, guided by world-class standards in mathematics, is necessary to transform the mathematics curriculum, teaching methods, and student assessments. The reform's success will also depend on the availability of greater opportunities for all students to learn mathematics and to use new technology. In addition, since the reform movement asks much of teachers, extensive and continuous staff development is needed. This includes courses in content to develop new and deeper knowledge of mathematics, courses in skills for facilitating learning, courses in new assessment methods, courses in implementing cooperative learning, and courses in working with diverse student populations.

In the end, the appropriate organizational structures must be in place to support the professional cooperation, planning, and school governance that in turn promote risk taking and reform and lead to a new state-of-the-art in mathematics.

EFFECTIVE SCHOOLS

The most important characteristics of effective schools are strong instructional leadership, a safe and orderly climate, school-wide emphasis on basic skills, high teacher expectations for student achievement, and continuous assessment of pupil progress.

One of the most important achievements of education research in the last 20 years has been identifying the factors that characterize effective schools, in particular the schools that have been especially successful in teaching basic skills to children from low-income families. Analysts first uncovered these characteristics when comparing the achievement levels of students from different urban schools. They labeled the schools with the highest achievement as "effective schools."

Schools with high student achievement and morale show certain characteristics:

• vigorous instructional leadership;
• a principal who makes clear, consistent, and fair decisions;
• an emphasis on discipline and a safe and orderly environment;
• instructional practices that focus on basic skills and academic achievement;
• collegiality among teachers in support of student achievement;
• teachers with high expectations that all their students can and will lear;, and
• frequent review of student progress.

Effective schools are places where principals, teachers, students, and parents agree on the goals, methods, and content of schooling. They are united in recognizing the importance of a coherent curriculum, public recognition for students who succeed, promoting a sense of school pride, and protecting school time for learning.

School Climate

Schools that encourage academic achievement focus on the importance of scholastic success and on maintaining order and discipline.

Good schools focus sharply on learning. In effective schools, the school climate – some call it the "learning environment" – puts academics first. Principals and teachers believe they can make a difference in what students learn. Teachers and students believe each student is capable of making significant academic progress. Students understand and agree that their first priority is to learn.

School activities reinforce these attitudes. Routines discourage disorder and disruptions. Teachers and principals protect the classroom from interruptions. Academic success is expected and rewarded. Public ceremonies honor student achievement.

Incoming students know the school's reputation and experienced students affirm the value placed on learning. Teacher morale is high and turnover is low. When there are openings, principals recruit and select teachers who share the school's goals and standards.

Principals work with teachers, students, parents, and community members to develop the school's learning environment. Once established, that learning environment becomes a durable part of the school's tradition.

Character Education

Good character is encouraged by surrounding students with good adult examples and by building upon natural occasions for learning and practicing good character. Skillful educators know how to organize their schools, classrooms, and lessons to foster such examples.

The home, the school, and the community all contribute to a child's character development. Children learn character traits such as honesty, courtesy, diligence, and respect for others, in part from examples set by their parents, teachers, peers, and the community as a whole.

Schools can reinforce good character by how they organize and present themselves, how the adults conduct themselves, and how standards for behavior and integrity are set and enforced. Positive character traits are reinforced through school activities that identify worthwhile achievements and exemplary behavior of students.

Educators become good role models through their professionalism, courtesy, cooperation, and by demanding top performance from their students. They maintain fair and consistent discipline policies, including matters of attendance, punctuality, and meeting assignment deadlines.

Teachers can use examples from life and literature to nurture qualities of good character and ethical behavior. History and biographies can provide role models, such as Martin Luther King and Helen Keller, to identify admirable character traits and to broaden students' horizons. Stories, fables, and poetry can reinforce enduring standards of conduct and create powerful images that enhance moral awareness and self-recognition. For example, *The Little Engine That Could* teaches young children perseverance; *A Christmas Carol* illustrates the ability to change from bad to good; *Captains Courageous* portrays a spoiled boy's transformation into a loyal friend; and *The Adventures of Huckleberry Finn* details a young boy's struggle with his conscience as he decides to reject the accepted norms of behavior to defend his friend Jim.

Libraries

The use of libraries enhances reading skills and encourages independent learning.

Research has shown that participating in library programs reinforces children's skills and interest in reading. Summer reading programs offered by public libraries, for example, reinforce reading skills learned during the school year. Library programs for pre-school children encourage children's interest in learning to read. Both types of programs provide many opportunities for reading, listening, and viewing materials.

Public and school libraries can enhance reading instruction by offering literature-based activities that stress the enjoyment of reading as well as reading skills. Hearing stories and participating in such activities help young children want to learn to read. These programs help children become more aware of the literary and cultural heritage that is necessary to help them understand much of what they will read and hear as they grow up.

Use of both public and school libraries encourages students to go beyond their textbooks to locate, explore, evaluate, and use ideas and information that enhance classroom instruction. Competent library personnel can help students learn how to seek information and give them opportunities to practice finding information.

Discipline

Schools contribute to their students' academic achievement by establishing, communicating, and enforcing fair and consistent discipline policies.

For sixteen of the last seventeen years, the public has identified discipline as the most serious problem facing its schools. Effective discipline policies contribute to the academic atmosphere by emphasizing the importance of regular attendance, promptness, respect for teachers and academic work, and good conduct.

Behavior and academic success go together. In one recent survey for example, high school sophomores who got "mostly A's" had one-third as many absences or incidents of tardiness per semester as those who got "mostly D's." The same students were 25 times more likely to have their homework done and 7 times less likely to have been in trouble with the law. Good behavior as a sophomore led to better grades and higher achievement as a senior.

The discipline policies of most successful schools share these traits:

• Discipline policies are aimed at actual problems, not rumors.

• All members of the school community are involved in creating a policy that reflects community values and is adapted to the needs of the school.

• Misbehavior is defined. Because not everyone agrees on what behavior is undesirable, defining problems is the first step in solving them. Students must know what kinds of behavior are acceptable and what kinds are not.

• Discipline policies are consistently enforced. Students must know the consequences of misbehavior, and they must believe they will be treated fairly.

• A readable and well-designed handbook is often used to inform parents and students about the school's discipline policy.

Attendance

A school staff that provides encouragement and personalized attention, and monitors daily attendance can reduce unexcused absences and class-cutting.

Absences are a major problem at all levels of school. Too many missed opportunities to learn can result in failure, dropping out, or both.

The school climate set by teachers, counselors, and administrators can significantly affect student attendance. Teachers who establish and communicate clear goals and high standards for performance and behavior, maintain discipline, allow as much learning time as possible, and consistently show support for their students have fewer attendance problems.

Good principals set the tone of schools by fostering a school climate that is conducive to teaching and learning. They address truancy problems by establishing preventive policies to monitor and control attendance. These policies are clearly communicated to students and are fairly and consistently enforced.

A school with an effective system for monitoring both daily and class attendance can identify potential dropouts early and then provide appropriate service to them.

An effective monitoring system also lets parents know when their children aren't in school. Research indicates that parents want to hear promptly if their children have unexcused absences. Some schools use staff members to check attendance records and phone the parents of absent students. Others have begun using automatic calling devices that leave a recorded message with parents. Schools using such devices report substantial increases in attendance.

Good attendance in school is another example of the connection of time and learning. Just as homework amplifies learning, regular attendance exposes students to a greater amount of academic content and instruction. Students, of course, must concentrate on their lessons in order to benefit from attendance.

Effective Principals

Successful principals establish policies that create an orderly environment and support effective instruction.

Effective principals have a vision of what a good school is and systematically strive to bring that vision to life in their schools. School improvement is their constant theme. They scrutinize existing practices to assure that all activities and procedures contribute to the quality of the time available for learning. They make sure teachers participate actively in this process. Effective principals, for example, make opportunities available for faculty to improve their own teaching and classroom management skills.

Good school leaders protect the school day for teaching and learning. They do this by keeping teachers' administrative chores and classroom interruptions to a minimum.

Effective principals visibly and actively support learning. Their practices create an orderly environment. Good principals make sure teachers have the necessary materials and the kind of assistance they need to teach well.

Effective principals also build morale in their teachers. They help teachers create a climate of achievement by encouraging new ideas; they also encourage teachers to help formulate school teaching policies and select textbooks. They try to develop community support for the school, its faculty, and its goals.

In summary, effective principals are experts at making sure time is available to learn, and at ensuring that teachers and students make the best use of that time.

Succeeding In A New School

When schools provide comprehensive orientation programs for students transferring from one school to another, they ease the special stresses and adjustment difficulties those students face. The result is apt to be improved student performance.

Each year approximately 30 percent of American public school enrollments consists of first-time students and transfer students. It takes most new students several months to adjust to a new school. In addition, teenagers face the normal stresses of adolescence. If a smooth transition to a new school does not take place, difficulties may develop that can affect a child throughout his school career.

An effective orientation program provides students and parents with basic information about the school, such as rules, policies and procedures, where to go and whom to see for what, etc. It encourages students to participate in extracurricular activities and provides them with good role models for appropriate school behavior.

A good program also stresses self-control and individual responsibility for actions and teaches students how to express dissatisfaction in socially acceptable ways and how to promote change.

An effective orientation program is a process rather than a single event; it addresses social and personal concerns as well as academic ones. Often, a deliberate attempt is made to integrate new students into the school by providing opportunities for them to relate to others and develop new friendships. Such programs give new students a sense of belonging and acceptance by other students.

A well-planned orientation program by the school can reduce the negative effects of transition and make adjusting to the new school an enriching experience rather than a traumatic one. Such a program can prevent potential problems related to academic achievement, attendance, and personal conduct.

INSTRUCTIONAL SUPPORT

Underachieving, or mildly handicapped students, can benefit most from remedial education when the lessons in those classes are closely coordinated with those in their regular classes.

Children with academic problems, especially in reading, are often referred to compensatory, remedial, or special education classes. These classes are supposed to offer them extra help in the subject with which they have difficulty. Remedial instruction is most successful when it is built upon and coordinated with a solid core curriculum. Therefore, the most beneficial remedial instruction for underachievers or mildly handicapped students is carefully and closely coordinated with regular classroom instruction. When such programs are not synchronized with what is going on in the regular classroom, the result is apt to be fragmented, even incoherent lessons for underachieving students.

Careful advance planning and close coordination of instruction help teachers give underachieving students more integrated and consistent lessons and, more importantly, provide additional instruction. For example, a remedial reading teacher could link a reading lesson to regular classroom activities by:
- focusing on the same skill, such as comprehension, that the regular classroom teacher is stressing;
- working on vocabulary by using words and concepts used in the child's science class that week;
- stressing the same reading strategies emphasized that day during the regular classroom reading group; and
- giving the child additional explanations and practice on concepts introduced in the regular classroom.

Organizing school staff into "teams" with common planning times and regular scheduled meetings helps regular classroom teachers and remedial teachers coordinate lessons and formulate a common sense of purpose and direction. In addition, such "team" planning and coordination helps teachers address the instructional and curricular needs of individual children.

COLLEGIALITY

Students benefit academically when their teachers share ideas, cooperate in activities, and assist one another's intellectual growth.

Although high student achievement is most likely in a school with high faculty morale and a sense of shared responsibility, most teachers are independent and believe that the responsibility of running their classrooms is theirs alone. In some studies, as many as 45 percent of the teachers report no contact with each other during the workday; another 32 percent say they have infrequent contact.

As a result, these teachers fail to share experience and ideas or to get support from their colleagues. Isolation may undermine effective instruction.

Good instruction flourishes when teachers collaborate in developing goals that emphasize student achievement. Effective schools have a climate of staff collegiality and use mutual support as a means of improving pupil achievement. School leaders in such schools set aside time for faculty interaction and provide specific opportunities for teachers and administrators to work together on such tasks as setting school policies, improving instructional practice, selecting textbooks, and strengthening discipline.

TEACHER SUPERVISION

Teachers welcome professional suggestions about improving their work, but they rarely receive them.

When supervisors comment constructively on teachers' specific skills, they help teachers become more effective and improve teachers' morale. Yet, typically, a supervisor visits a teacher's classroom only once a year and makes only general comments about the teacher's performance. This relative lack of specific supervision contributes to low morale, teacher absenteeism, and high faculty turnover.

Supervision that strengthens instruction and improves teachers' morale has these elements:

• agreement between supervisor and teacher on the specific skills and practices that characterize effective teaching;
• frequent observation by the supervisor to see if the teacher is using these skills and practices;
• a meeting between supervisor and teacher to discuss the supervisor's impressions;
• agreement by the supervisor and teacher on areas for improvement; and
• a specific plan for improvement, jointly constructed by teacher and supervisor.

Principals who are good supervisors make themselves available to help teachers. They make teachers feel they can come for help without being branded failures.

Main-Streaming Children With Special Needs

Many children who are physically handicapped or have emotional or learning problems can be given an appropriate education in well supported regular classes and schools.

In the past, educators often assumed that some children needed "special" education that could be provided only in special places – such as resource rooms, special classes, or special schools. In some cases, handicapped children were removed from their own homes and local schools and placed in special residential schools. Now more of them are learning well in regular classes and schools.

Several instructional practices have proven effective in serving students with special needs in regular classrooms and schools. When teachers have children work on assignments and projects together, handicapped and non-handicapped students benefit from each other's insight and expertise. Teachers encourage independence by creating active learning opportunities where students initiate projects from course work and then complete them individually or with other students. Computer assisted instruction is especially useful for students who need extra instructional support. And, lessons and units of study which are structured but individually paced offer advantages to all students and make the regular classroom effective for children with handicaps – especially when special education and school psychologists work together with regular teachers.

Regular teachers can support each other by meeting to discuss children's problems, provide instructional suggestions and support, and increase teacher skills and comfort in dealing with children with special needs. Such meetings provide a forum where teachers can use their creativity and problem solving abilities, share their skills and knowledge, and help each other cope with classroom problems.

School-to-Work Transition

Handicapped high school students who seek them are more likely to find jobs after graduation when schools prepare them for careers and when private sector businesses provide on-the-job training.

Many individuals with disabilities, especially those handicapped youth who do not attend college, are chronically unemployed. Programs and services to help them get jobs are fragmented. There is little coordination between employment agencies and schools or programs that offer compensatory, social or vocational help.

Successful school-to-work transition programs have been developed that improve coordination between school staffs, state agencies and community employers. Under these programs, special education teachers help students explore career possibilities and develop job-seeking skills and work ethics. Vocational educators cooperate with special education teachers to adapt their instruction to the needs of the students.

Such programs find jobs for students by offering prospective employers incentives such as pre-screened employees, on-the-job assistance with trainees, and most importantly, wage stipends. Employment and rehabilitation staff provide expertise on a referral basis. Additional resources are needed to cover the schools' excess cost of developing jobs and offering training stipends.

History

Skimpy requirements and declining enrollments in history classes are contributing to a decline in students' knowledge of the past.

Earlier generations of American students commonly learned the history of American institutions, politics, and systems of government, as well as some of the history of Greece, Rome, Europe, and the rest of the world. Today, most states require the study of only American history and other course work in social studies. Indications are that students now know and understand less about history.

In most state requirements for high school graduation, a choice is offered between history on the one hand and courses in social science and contemporary social issues on the other. Most high school students, even those in the academic track, take only one history course. Students enroll in honors courses in history at less than half the rate they enroll for honors courses in English and science. Typically, requirements have also declined for writing essays, producing research based papers, and reading original sources. Similar declines are reported in the requirements for such reasoning skills as evaluating sources of information, drawing conclusions, and constructing logical arguments.

As a result, students know too little about the past. The National Assessment of Education Progress has pilot-tested the knowledge of 17 year olds about American history. The preliminary results of this study indicate that two-thirds of the students tested could not place the Civil War within the period 1850-1900; half could not identify Winston Churchill or Joseph Stalin.

The decline in the study of history may hinder students from gaining an historical perspective on contemporary life.

Cultural Literacy

Students read more fluently and with greater understanding if they have knowledge of the world and their culture, past and present. Such knowledge and understanding is called cultural literacy.

In addition to their knowledge of the physical world, students' knowledge of their culture determines how they will grasp the meaning of what they read. Students read and understand passages better when the passages refer to events, people and places – real or fictional – with which the students are familiar.

Students' understanding of the subtleties and complexities of written information depends on how well they understand cultural traditions, attitudes, values, conventions, and connotations. The more literate students are in these ways, the better prepared they will be to read and understand serious books, magazines, and other challenging material.

Most school teachers, college professors, journalists, and social commentators agree that the general knowledge of American students is too low, and getting lower. Surveys document great gaps in students' basic knowledge of geography, history, literature, politics, and democratic principles. Teaching is hindered if teachers cannot count on their students sharing a body of knowledge, references, and symbols.

Every society maintains formal and informal mechanisms to transmit understanding of its history, literature, and political institutions from one generation to the next. A shared knowledge of these elements of our past helps foster social cohesion and a sense of national community and pride.

In the United States, the national community comprises diverse groups and traditions. Together they have created a rich cultural heritage. Cultural literacy not only enables students to read better and gain new knowledge; it enables them to understand the shared heritage, institutions, and values that draw Americans together.

FOREIGN LANGUAGE

The best way to learn a foreign language in school is to start early and to study it intensively over many years.

The percentage of high school students studying foreign language declined from 73 percent in 1915 to 15 percent in 1979. Some states and schools are beginning to emphasize foreign language study. However, even with this new emphasis, most students who take a foreign language study it for 2 years or less in high school and do not learn to communicate with it effectively.

Students are most likely to become fluent in a foreign language if they begin studying it in elementary school and continue studying it for 6 to 8 years. Although older students may learn foreign languages faster than younger ones, students who start early are likely to become more proficient and to speak with a near-native accent.

"Total immersion" language study programs in the United States and Canada that begin instruction in the early grades and teach all subjects in the foreign language have been highly successful in teaching all students both the language and regular academic subjects.

If new foreign language requirements are really to improve students' language competence, experience has shown that schools will need to:
• find qualified teachers;
• set consistent goals;
• select appropriate materials; and
• continue a coherent program of instruction from elementary to junior to senior high school.

RIGOROUS COURSES

The stronger the emphasis on academic courses, the more advanced the subject matter, and the more rigorous the textbooks, the more high school students learn. Subjects that are learned mainly in school rather than at home, such as science and math, are most influenced by the number and kind of courses taken.

Students often handicap their intellectual growth by avoiding difficult courses. In order to help young people make wise course choices, schools are increasingly requiring students to take courses that match their grade level and abilities; schools are also seeing to it that the materials used in those courses are intellectually challenging.

The more rigorous the course of study, the more a student achieves, within the limits of his capacity. Student achievement also depends on how much the school emphasizes a subject and the amount of time spent on it; the more time expended, the higher the achievement. Successful teachers encourage their students' best efforts.

ACCELERATION

Advancing gifted students at a faster pace results in their achieving more than similarly gifted students who are taught at a normal rate.

Advocates of accelerating the education of gifted and talented students believe that this practice furnishes the extra challenge these students need to realize their full potential. Critics believe acceleration may result in emotional and social stress if a child is unable to get along with older students. Some, concerned about those who remain behind, characterize acceleration as unfair or undemocratic.

Research evidence generally supports acceleration. When abler students are moved ahead in school, they typically learn more in less time than students of the same age and ability who are taught at the conventional rate. Accelerated students score a full grade level or more higher on achievement tests than their conventionally placed schoolmates. Some may score several years ahead of their schoolmates.

Acceleration does not damage students' attitudes about school subjects. Nor do accelerated students necessarily become drudges or bookworms; they ordinarily continue to participate in extracurricular activities. Such students often become more sure about their occupational goals.

Accelerated students perform as well as talented but older students in the same grade. Despite being younger, accelerated students are able to capitalize on their abilities and achieve beyond the level available to them had they remained in the lower grade.

Extracurricular Activities

High school students who complement their academic studies with extracurricular activities gain experience that contributes to their success in college.

High school class rank and test scores are the best predictors of academic success in college, but involvement sustained over time in one or two extracurricular activities contributes to overall achievement in college. On the other hand, when these activities become ends in themselves, academic performance may suffer.

Students who participate in extracurricular activities gain some significant advantages. Among them are:

- opportunities for recognition, personal success, and broader experience to complement their academic achievement;
- the chance to develop intellectual, social, cultural, and physical talents to round out their academic education; and
- the opportunity to extend the boundaries of the classroom by acquiring direct experience with the content and worth of a subject; for example, when drama club members study and present the plays of Shakespeare, or when debaters gain practice in applied logic, research, and public presentations.

Although such activities as athletics are less clearly related to academic goals, they do provide opportunities for physical growth and self-discipline. Indeed, all these activities can extend the range of experience that schools can offer.

But when extracurricular activities get out of balance, problems can arise, as when high school athletes treat sports as an alternative to learning rather than an addition to it. Distracted by the prestige they earn in sports, student athletes may fail to prepare adequately for the academic requirements of college or the work place. This situation has worsened in recent years, and many abuses have come to light, such as lowering (or winking at) the academic requirements for sports eligibility. There have been recent attempts to rectify this situation by reinstating academic criteria as a condition for participation in all extracurricular activities.

Work Experience

When students work more than 15 to 20 hours per week, their grades may suffer. They can benefit, however, from limited out-of-school work.

The proportion of teenagers holding part time jobs has increased dramatically recently. Some students work because they need the money; others because they want to have adult style responsibilities and experiences. But holding a part time job for more than 15 to 20 hours per week during the school year may actually do more harm than good. Working longer than that often accompanies a decline in school performance and diminished interest in school.

Students can benefit from jobs, however, if work hours are limited, the experience is well selected, and the job does not interfere with their school work. Such jobs help improve knowledge about the work place, foster positive attitudes and habits, and open up possibilities for careers. Although many students find jobs on their own, some join school sponsored job programs. Such programs, when well conceived:

- Manage the number of hours students work, thus controlling the one aspect of work experience most likely to harm students' grades.
- Carefully monitor and guide the work experience, coordinating the efforts of students and employers so that both benefit. Good programs give students opportunities to relate their work experience to other school activities.
- Make sure the job meets the student's needs. Some jobs, for example, may give students an opportunity to experiment with different career possibilities; others may give students chances to acquire and practice technical skills.

PREPARATION FOR WORK

Business leaders report that students with solid basic skills and positive work attitudes are more likely to find and keep jobs than students with vocational skills alone.

As new technologies make old job skills obsolete, the best vocational education will be solid preparation in reading, writing, mathematics, and reasoning. In the future, American workers will acquire many of their job skills in the work place, not in school. They will need to be able to master new technologies and upgrade their skills to meet specialized job demands. Men and women who have weak basic skills, or who cannot readily master new skills to keep pace with change, may be only marginally employed over their lifetimes.

Business leaders recommend that schools raise academic standards. They point to the need for remedial programs to help low-achieving students and to reduce dropping out.

Business leaders stress that the school curriculum should emphasize literacy, mathematics, and problem-solving skills. They believe schools should emphasize such personal qualities as self-discipline, reliability, perseverance, teamwork, accepting responsibility, and respect for the rights of others. These characteristics will serve all secondary students well, whether they go on to college or directly into the world of work.